Maurice Purcell Fitz-Gerald

The Crowned Hippolytus of Euripides

Together with a Selection from the Pastoral and Lyric Poets of Greece

Maurice Purcell Fitz-Gerald

The Crowned Hippolytus of Euripides
Together with a Selection from the Pastoral and Lyric Poets of Greece

ISBN/EAN: 9783744777735

Printed in Europe, USA, Canada, Australia, Japan

Cover: Foto ©Thomas Meinert / pixelio.de

More available books at **www.hansebooks.com**

THE

CROWNED HIPPOLYTUS

OF EURIPIDES,

TOGETHER WITH

A SELECTION FROM THE PASTORAL AND LYRIC
POETS OF GREECE,

Translated into English Verse

BY

MAURICE PURCELL FITZ-GERALD.

LONDON:

CHAPMAN AND HALL, 193 PICCADILLY.

1867.

LONDON :

ROBSON AND SON, GREAT NORTHERN PRINTING WORKS,

PANCRAS ROAD, N.W.

My best thanks are due to W. BODHAM DONNE, Esq. for his great kindness in looking over the sheets of this little volume as they passed through the press, and for allowing me to benefit by his refined taste and accomplished scholarship.

CONTENTS.

HIPPOLYTUS.

THESEUS was son of Æthra and Poseidon, and king of Athens. He married Hippolyta, one of the Amazons, and had by her Hippolytus, who was remarkable for beauty and continence. And when she died he took for second wife Phædra, a native of Crete, daughter of Minos king of Crete, and of Pasiphaë. And because he had slain Pallas, one of his kinsfolk, Theseus fled with his wife to Trœzen, where it happened that Hippolytus was being educated in the house of Pittheus. And so soon as Phædra beheld the youth she fell headlong into hot desire for him ; and not to escape scot-free therefrom, but rather to fulfil to the utmost the wrath of Aphroditè, who, having determined to destroy Hippolytus for his chastity, planned the accomplishment of her purpose by exciting a raging love for him in Phædra's heart. And after concealing her malady for a long time she was constrained to reveal it to her nurse, who had promised to be her helper. And the nurse, doing as she thought best, informed the young man. And when Phædra learned of his rage and exasperation, she reproached the nurse angrily for what she had done, and went and hanged herself. And Theseus arrived about the same time, and hastened to take down her that was hanged, and found attached to her person a writing-tablet, in which Hippolytus was accused of treachery and of having brought her to destruction. And Theseus believed what was written, and ordered Hippolytus into exile, and cursed him, and prayed against him to Poseidon his father ; and the god hearkened to his prayer, and destroyed Hippolytus. But Artemis appeared, and explained to Theseus severally the things that had happened, and made them clear to him ; and she excused Phædra from blame, and she comforted Theseus, now that he was bereft of his wife and of his son, and she promised that national honours should be paid to Hippolytus.

APHRODITÉ.

HIPPOLYTUS.

ATTENDANTS.

CHORUS OF TRŒZENIAN WOMEN.

NURSE.

PHÆDRA.

MESSENGER.

THESEUS.

SECOND MESSENGER.

ARTEMIS.

HIPPOLYTUS.

APHRODITÉ.

I AM no nameless deity, for men
At many a shrine lift hands, and hail me Cypris,—
And hosts of heaven, and peoples of the sea,
And whosoever house within the bounds
Of Atlas-shouldered earth, and see the sun :
And those that reverence my power I favour,
But I confound all who think-scorn of me.
For even divinity is fashioned thus—
It joys in mortal honours. I will show
Briefly my word's true meaning. For see here,
This son of Theseus, this Hippolytus,
This offspring of the Amazon, this fruit
Of holy Pittheus' lessons, this sole one
Of all the dwellers on Trœzenian soil
Calls me most hateful, most detestable
Of deities ; also he doth refuse
The marriage-bed, and spurns the nuptial knot,

Honouring Apollo's sister Artemis,
The first of heavenly ones in his esteem ;
And ever roams he in her virgin train,
In intercourse too close for mortal man,
Through the pale yellow woods, with fleetest hounds
Scaring the wild beasts that infest the land.
Yet this I grudge him not : it harms not me ;
But what *has* harmed me I will visit on him
This very day, and without much ado,
My plans long since provided to this end.

　　For once when he had travelled from the house
Of Pittheus, in the holy mysteries
Of Attica to be initiate,
Phædra, his father's high-born consort, saw him ;
Forthwith terrible love possessed her heart,
For so I worked it : and before she came
To Trœzen, close beside Athené's cliff
That overlooks this land, she raised a fane
To Cypris, love-struck with an absent love,
And named, in honour of Hippolytus,
Unto all future times the goddess-shrine.
But after Theseus fled the taint of blood
And curse of the Pallantidæ, and left
Cecropian soil, and voyaged to this land,
Vowing a twelvemonth's exile for his crime,
And she, his wife, voyaged with him ; then, alas !
Thenceforth a thing of grief, love-pierced to the heart
Piteously in silence she wastes away.
And none of her attendants know the cause ;

But not in this way must this love fall through :
I will tell the tale to Theseus ;—every jot
Shall be revealed, and him, my enemy,
The curses of his father shall destroy,
According to the power by ocean-king
Poseidon given, that Theseus unto him
Three times might pray, thrice pray for nought in vain.
And she, all high-born as she is, she dies,
Phædra must die { I reck not of her death
In face of paying such vengeance on my foes
As may appease my wronged divinity.}
　　Now, for I see advancing hitherwards
This son of Theseus, lately from the chase,
Will I move off.　Much people follows him :
Shouts his attendant band, and lifts the hymn
To Artemis.　But little does he know
The gates of the grave are open, and the sun
He looks on he shall never look on more.

HIPPOLYTUS.

Follow, follow me ;
Raise the choral melody
To our heavenly mistress,
Zeus-descended Artemis,
　Whose care are we !

ATTENDANTS.

Maiden of stateliness, maiden of might,
Hail, O hail !
Zeus' and Latona's daughter bright,
Hail, O hail !

Fairest by far of the virgin-band
　　That in heaven above
In the wide-spreading halls doth stand
　　Of the golden dome of Jove.
　　　Artemis, Artemis !

HIPPOLYTUS.

　　Hail, maiden fairest,
　　Hail, maiden rarest
　　Of all the Olympian band.
　　　Artemis, Artemis !

Mistress, this flower-crown have I wreathed for thee,
The enwoven blossoms of an unmown meadow,
Where neither shepherd dares to lead his flocks
To pasture, nor a scythe hath ever come ;
But always in the springtime flits the bee
O'er the untrodden herbage, and with streams
Of freshening dew Aurora feeds its growth.
Not those trained to be chaste, but those whose nature
In all alike has reached to chastity,
May pluck these flowers, denied to the impure.
Then, mistress loved, from a most reverent hand
Accept this garland for thy golden hair.
This is my bliss, alone of humankind
To live with thee, to mix my words with thine,
To hear thy voice, although thy face is hid.
Thus has my life begun, thus may it end.

ATTENDANT.

Prince,—for the gods alone we own as lords,—
Wouldst take from me a word of timely counsel ?

HIPPOLYTUS.

With right good will—else were we scantly wise.

ATTENDANT.

Know'st thou what rule is laid on mortal men?

HIPPOLYTUS.

I know not—nor the purport of thy question.

ATTENDANT.

Pride to detest and partiality.

HIPPOLYTUS.

Right; but where is the proud who is not hated?

ATTENDANT.

Stop :—is there any grace in courtesy?

HIPPOLYTUS.

Much, much; and profit too at little cost.

ATTENDANT.

Think'st thou that with the gods the same holds good?

HIPPOLYTUS.

Yes, if we mortals use the laws of gods.

ATTENDANT.

Why then in prayer pass over one dread power?

HIPPOLYTUS.

What power? take heed, for fear thy tongue go tripping.

ATTENDANT.

The power that stands before thy threshold—Cypris.

HIPPOLYTUS.

I am spotless. I salute her from afar.

ATTENDANT.

Yet she is honoured, and in much esteem.

HIPPOLYTUS.

Some with this god and some with that have dealings.

ATTENDANT.

May'st thou be blest with a right-thinking mind !

HIPPOLYTUS.

No god for me that asks a midnight worship.

ATTENDANT.

Young man, each power must have its chosen honours.

HIPPOLYTUS.

Hence now, attendants ; see the feast be set
Within the palace : when the chase is done
Welcome the well-spread board ; also take care
To groom my coursers, that, the banquet ended,
Unto my chariot I may harness them
And exercise them fitly. For thy Cypris
Thou talkest of, I bid her a good day.

ATTENDANT.

But we, no imitators of the young,
In prudent language as befits our station,
Will lift the voice of prayer, O mighty Cypris,
Before thy image ; and thou wilt forgive
The foolish babbling of intemperate youth,
And what thou hearest thou wilt set aside
As if thou heard'st it not ; needs must great gods
Be wise above the foolishness of men.

CHORUS.

They tell me of a cliff that Ocean washes,
    Whence sweet streams downwards pour;
And many an urn-refreshing fountain flashes
    From rift and craggy scaur:
There a loved friend of mine was wont to lave
Her crimson vestments in the beaded wave,
And spread them where the torrid glow
Flames on a rib of rock below.

Thence the first rumour reached me that my queen,
    Her fair hair lightly veiled,
Lies on her palace-bed alone, unseen,
    By wasting pains assailed:
Three days hath Ceres' bounty been withstood,
Three days her fair lips have been pure from food;
From some dark sorrow fain to die,
She hastes to a bourne of misery.

O, surely by some god thou art inspired,
    Or Pan, or Hecaté,
Or by the awful Corybantes fired,
Or the mighty Mother's mountain company.
Or, for some votive rites thou didst not pay,
The goddess-huntress bids thee pine away;
For she flits across the mainland and the mere,
Where the salt waves curl in eddies she is near!

Or does some stealthy rival of thy bed
    Corrupt the Erechthid chief,
Thy noble spouse; or has some sailor sped
From the Cretan shore, a messenger of grief,
And to the welcome shelter of this bay
Voyaged, perchance, with tidings of dismay,
And does she with her sorrow sore opprest
Lie prisoned to the pillows of unrest?

Ah! surely in these wayward female natures
Lives harmony of inharmonious features;
The helpless years of child-bearing distress,
The helpless years of foolishness!
I mind the day this blast of fate
Swept through my womb distemperate.
But then to her that soothes the matron's pain,
To Artemis, the heavenly archeress,
I cried, nor cried in vain.
And ever walks she in the heavenly train,
And ever will I worship at her fane.

But see the ancient nurse before the door
Has led her from her chamber-floor.
And look upon her dismal brow
How the cloud of grief doth grow.
My heart beats fast to hear the tale
    Of all my queen's sad woes;
      Wherefore her cheeks have lost the rose,
Have faded, and have turned to deathly pale.

NURSE.

Alas for mortal woes!
Alas for fell disease!
What shall I do for thee, what leave undone?
See here the bright light of the sun,
    Feel here the open breeze,
The pillows of thy sick-couch spread
    Without the gates invite repose.
Ever thy speech had this refrain,
    "Hither, O, hither let me be led!"
And now thou wilt hasten soon again
    Back to thy weary bed!
So quickly is thy frame upset,
At everything so sure to fret,
All that thou hast thou dost detest,
And all thou hast not ever seems the best.
Better be sick than be the sick one's nurse;
Sickness is sickness, nothing worse;
Nursing is sorrow in double kind,
Sorrow of toiling hands, sorrow of troubled mind.
Our life is blasted all with sorrow's curse,
    Our troubles know no healing.
But if in lands beyond
Is something better than this life, it lies
    In folded shroud of darkness all-concealing;
Therefore of this are we so madly fond,
Because its glitter doth allure our eyes,
But of that other are we all in doubt,

Of realms beneath the earth is no revealing :
But with much fables are we tossed about.

PHÆDRA.

Lift up my body,
    Straighten my head,
    Hold up the hands
    And arms of the dead ;
The joints of my limbs are loosened, the veil on my
    brow is like lead.
Take it off, take it off, let the clustering curls on my
    shoulders be spread!

NURSE.

O, courage, child ; O, yield not so
Thy life to unremitting woe :
A quiet frame, a high-born will,
Will likeliest stem the flood of ill ;
For trouble is the doom of men below.

PHÆDRA.

Ay me ! could I drink
    The pure lymph issuing
    From the dewy brink
    Of a crystal spring !
Could I lie in the poplar shadow,
Could I stretch my limbs in repose, and rest in the
    verdurous meadow !

NURSE.

Nay, sweet one, mourn not so aloud,
Such language must not reach the crowd ;

Thy heedless speech is borne along,
And frenzy lords it o'er thy tongue.

PHÆDRA.

Send me, send me to the mountain; I will wander to
    the wood,
Where the dogs amid the pine-copse track and tear the
    wild-beast's brood;
I will hang upon his traces where the dappled roe-buck
    bounds;
I yearn, by all the gods I yearn to halloa to the hounds,
To poise the lance of Thessaly above my yellow hair,
And to loose my hand and lightly launch the barbèd
    point through air!

NURSE.

Why trouble, child, for things like this?
The chase is nought to thee, I wis:
    Why crave the fountain's plash?
Rises above these towers a hill
    Where never-ceasing torrents dash:
There may'st thou drink at will.

PHÆDRA.

    Queen of the ocean-lake,
        Queen of the gymnast-courses,
    Where the earth doth shake
        With the thunder of horses.
O Artemis, if I could ride with thee, and rein
The Adrian coursers bounding o'er the plain!

NURSE.

Another wish to folly leaning!
Another utterance without meaning!
First on the mountain wouldst thou stand,
For hunting all afire,
And now fleet steeds are thy desire
Upon the unrippled sand.
This needs much gift of seer to say
What god is leading thee astray,
And scaring reason from her throne away.

PHÆDRA.

O misery!
What have I done?
Where have my better senses gone?
I am mad; some vengeful god presses me sore.
Ah! woe is me!
Good mother, cover up my head once more:
I blush for all that I have said.
Hide, hide my head.
The hot tears trickle from my eyes,
My eyelids droop for shame:
'Tis when the better mind returns
The bitter grief begins;
O, madness is an awful name,
And he is happier far who dies
In ignorance, before he learns
His sorrows and his sins!

NURSE.

I hide thee. Aye ; but when will death come hide
My weary limbs ? for how much length of days
Makes me see life in many diverse ways.
The bonds of human friendship should be tied
Not tightly, not to chain the inmost soul,
The heart's affections held in light control,
Now closelier drawn, now coldly set aside.
But for one heart to bear the grief of two,
As I bear hers and mine, is heavy measure.
Such nice attention to steer safely through
The sea of life brings shipwreck more than treasure.
And storms the bulwarks of a healthy frame ;
Therefore excess to me less worthy seems
Than strength that never struggles to extremes ;
And wisdom of the sages speaks the same.

CHORUS.

Time-honoured trusty servant of our queen,
We see her piteous plight, but of the cause
We wot not, for there is no evidence ;
This would we ask, and fain would learn from thee.

NURSE.

I know not. I have asked. She will not answer.

CHORUS.

Nor how came a beginning of her sorrows ?

NURSE.

'Tis all the same. She hides it all in silence.

CHORUS.

How pale she looks, and wasted all to nothing !

NURSE.

Could she look else after a three-days fast ?

CHORUS.

Fasts she from misery, or desire to die ?

NURSE.

To die.   To be rid of life she tastes not food.

CHORUS.

Marvellous, were her lord with this content !

NURSE.

She hides her griefs ; she vows she has no harm.

CHORUS.

Infers he not from tokens of her face ?

NURSE.

He would, but now is absent from the land.

CHORUS.

Dost thou not urge and press her, in attempt
To learn the malady of her distraught mind ?

NURSE.

I have striven in every way with none effect.
Nor even now will I relax my zeal,
And ye yourselves shall bear me present witness
Of what I am towards my unhappy queen.

    Come now, sweet child, forget our former talk,
Let each forget, and be of better cheer,
Unknit that gloomy brow, and turn aside

The current of thy thought, and, as for me,
If I said aught before that was not well,
I do renounce it, and will cast about
For fitter speech. Look now, if thy disease
Is such that thou dost shame to mention it,
These women here will find a remedy.
But if it may be spoken of to men,
O call the leech, and let him hear the whole.
Well :—silent still?—silence hath no place here :
Either correct me, if I speak not true,
Or add consent, if I have spoken well.
Say something :—look towards me :—woe is me!
Good women, all this labour is in vain !
We are just as far as ever from the truth.
No words of mine could soften her before,
No words of mine can make her listen now.

Know this at least,—although the sea itself
Is not so stubborn,—that if thou wilt die,
And leave thy children, they will have no place
Within their father's halls ; and this I swear
By that horse-taming queen, that Amazon
Who bore one that will lord it o'er thy race,—
Base-born, but noble-souled ; thou knowest him well,—
Hippolytus.

PHÆDRA.

Ah, woe's me !

NURSE.

Touches thee this?

C

PHÆDRA.

O mother, thou hast crushed me : by the gods
I pray thee speak not of that man again.

NURSE.

Look now : thy sense is sound, yet moves thee not
To save thy life and be thy children's helper.

PHÆDRA.

I love them ; I am tossed by other fates.

NURSE.

Surely thy hands are undefiled by blood ?

PHÆDRA.

My hands are pure : the taint is in my heart.

NURSE.

Did an enemy work the wrong and plant it there ?

PHÆDRA.

A friend ;—unwilling foe, unwilling victim !

NURSE.

Is it Theseus then has sinned a sin against thee ?

PHÆDRA.

Pray I be found not sinning against him !

NURSE.

What this strange woe, that makes thee long for death ?

PHÆDRA.

Let me go sin,—I sin not against thee.

NURSE.

Not with my will :—I will die with thee rather.

PHÆDRA.

How now? with force dost fasten to my hands?

NURSE.

Aye, from thy knees too I will not give hold.

PHÆDRA.

'Twere woe to thee, poor friend, heard'st thou my woe.

NURSE.

Could I have greater woe than loss of thee?

PHÆDRA.

'Twere death.   Therefore my action brings me honour.

NURSE.

Yet hid'st thou things of honour from my prayer?

PHÆDRA.

Out of evil I am working to bring good.

NURSE.

And so by open speech would prove thy honour.

PHÆDRA.

Get hence; by the gods, I charge thee drop my hand.

NURSE.

No, for thou dost refuse a proper boon.

PHÆDRA.

I grant it; I revere thy suppliant hand.

NURSE.

Now am I dumb: henceforth thou lead'st the speech.

PHÆDRA.

Alas, poor mother, what a love inflamed thee!

NURSE.

Love for the bull mean'st thou, or what beside ?

PHÆDRA.

Thou too, poor sister, bride of Dionysus !

NURSE.

What ails thee, child, so to defame thy kindred ?

PHÆDRA.

And I the third, how piteously I perish !

NURSE.

Now do I shudder.   Whither will these words tend ?

PHÆDRA.

Thence springs my misery—from no later source.

NURSE.

I know no more of what I wish to know.

PHÆDRA.
Alas !
Thyself must speak the words that I should speak.

NURSE.

I am no seer to read these riddles right.

PHÆDRA.

What is this called by men the being in love ?

NURSE.

The sweetest joy, the bitterest grief in one.

PHÆDRA.

I have felt them both,—the bitter and the sweet.

NURSE.

How now ?—thou lovest : whom then dost thou love ?

PHÆDRA.

Him,—whosoe'er he be,—the Amazon's son—

NURSE.

Hippolytus, say'st thou?

PHÆDRA.

Thou sayest it, not I.

NURSE.

Woe, woe! what will come next? child, thou hast killed
  me:
Women, this is unbearable: to live
Is hateful: hateful is the day, the sun
I look upon is hateful. I will hurl
My body to destruction; I will die,
I will be rid of life; farewell, farewell,
No more will I be seen. Not even the chaste
'Scape evil loves, albeit they seek them not.
So then this Cypris is no deity,
But something greater than a deity,
That ruins her and me and the whole house.

CHORUS.

Hast heard, ay me!
Hast heard our mistress wail unheard-of woe,
  Unheard-of misery?
Sooner to Hades let me go
Than that thou wreak the purpose of thy mind.
O woe, woe, woe!
O grief thou common nurse of humankind!
O pitiful in thy distress!

Lost ! lost ! thou hast brought dark ills to light of day !
What have these passing hours in store ?
What new woes heavily on us press
The fates will soon complete.
But as for thee, O hapless child of Crete,
No need to question more
'Gainst whom the Cyprian power will waste itself away!

PHÆDRA.

Women of Trœzen, that do dwell around
This extreme threshold of Pelopian soil,
Oft have I mused and pondered heretofore
In the long hours of night, how human life
Is wrecked and ruined ; for it seems to me
Men do not sin because their nature bids them,
(For the right path is clearly seen by many)
But we must face the question in this wise :
We know the good, we can distinguish it,
But will not strive to do it ; some from sloth,
And some from preference before the good
Of lower pleasures ; for there are in life
Pleasures diverse : pleasure of idle talk ;
And quiet ease, a vice most fascinating ;
And shame, which is twofold—one unfraught with ill,
The other filling homes with heavy grief.
Nor, were for each the moment clearly shewn,
Would selfsame letters fold a double meaning.
Therefore I deemed, after much forethought given,
There was no witchery that could corrupt

And overturn my mind from its firm base;
And I will show the tenor of my thought.

When love first pierced me, I looked all around
How best to bear it, and thenceforth began
To muffle up my malady in silence.
For who would trust his tongue, which can reprove
The wandering thoughts of others, but itself
Inherits from itself a thousand ills?
Next I bethought me I might bear the frenzy,
If that by chastity I vanquished it.
And last, if none of these would aught avail
To master passion, I resolved on death
As best of all. None can dispute my counsel.
If I do good, I would not wish to hide it;
If I do ill, I want not witnesses.
I knew the cause, the act, were each disgraceful;
I knew, from promptings of my woman-wit,
The common voice would loathe them. Perish she,
Perish a thousand times, who first began
To stain the marriage-bed with alien loves.
Alas, the daughters of a noble house
First sinned this sin! And when the better sort
Take evil for their good, be sure the base
Will cling to it as supreme excellence.
Also I loathe who prate of chastity,
But slily joy in ventures of no fame;
Who look,—O sea-born Cypris, can it be?—
Into the faces of their sleeping lords,
Nor tremble lest the darkness, their accomplice,

Or the remotest chambers of the house,
Should waken into utterance of their crime.
This, friends, would be my death, if I were found
(Which may the gods avert !) dishonouring
My husband, and my children whom I bore.
O in our noble Athens may they dwell,
Free men, exulting in free confidence,
And honoured for an honoured mother's sake !
For knowledge of a parent's evil deeds
Enslaves a man, strong-hearted though he be.
This, this alone is victor over life,—
Clear conscience, and possession of uprightness.
But for the wicked the day comes when time,
Like a young virgin, holds the mirror up,
Wherein they are glassed.—Let me not be of them !

CHORUS.

Yes, chastity is everywhere becoming,
And among mortals bears a good report.

NURSE.

Mistress, at first the news of thy mischance
Afflicted me with strange and sudden fear.
Now I perceive my error ; and somehow
The second thoughts of mortals prove the wiser.
For thou hast suffered nothing out of bounds,
Nothing unheard of ; but the goddess-fires
Have flamed upon thee. Sayest thou, thou lovest?
What wonder? many a mortal does the same.
Then for the cause of love wilt lose thy life?

No profit then for any folk who love,
Or now or after, if they needs must die.
For Cypris, in the torrent of her strength,
Cannot be borne; whoso submits to her
She gently sways ; but him who prides himself,
And bids defiance, look you, she enthrals,
And, as she pleases, makes a mock of him.
For Cypris roams through æther, and her foot
Falls on the ocean-billow; and from her
Spring all things; she it is who sows, she gives
That sweet desire whence we who live on earth
Derive our being. Those who ponder o'er
The writings of old time, and with the Muse
Hold frequent converse, know well long ago
How Zeus wooed Semelé; for love's sweet sake
How radiant Eös snatched young Cephalus
To consort with the gods; yet still in heaven
They dwell, nor fly the presences divine,
Who yield, I ween, to fate, and likewise love.
But thou, thou wilt not yield? yet must thy sire
Have got thee by fixed laws, or by the will
Of other gods, if these laws please thee not.
How many, think'st thou, with much store of sense,
Seeing their beds defiled, seem not to see?
How many fathers aid their children's slips,
And second Cypris?—for this saying holds
Among the wise—'Faults should be covered up.'
Men must not make an endless toil of life.
The roof, with which this house is vaulted o'er

Need not be spick and span; and thinkest thou
From such a sea of fate to swim dryshod?
Know, mortal as thou art, that if thy blessings
Outnumber thy ill-fates, thou art thrice blest.
So, daughter dear, curb thy distempered mind,
And stay thy impious wish; for nothing less
Than impious is the aim of mortal man
To set himself above the immortal gods.
Endure thy love; the gods have willed it so;
And in thy weakness cast about how best
To bear it to its ending; there are charms,
And there are spells of melting blandishment.
Be sure some remedy will come to light.
For if we women failed to find the means,
'Twere long indeed ere men discovered them.

CHORUS.

Phædra, her words do meet the present case
More fitly, though my praise is left for thine.
Albeit this praise is harder far to bear,
And sadder far to hear, than all her sophisms.

PHÆDRA.

This is it, this too fine-spun arguing
That roots up populous cities, and destroys
Whole houses; for we want not flattering words
To please the ear, but speech whose quality
May lead to noble action in the hearers.

NURSE.

Why this high moral phrasing? 'tis no time

For seemly talk; a man, a man's the stake;
And we must cast about who shall convey
The plain straightforward message of thy passion.
If this mischance had not befallen thee,
Thee a chaste wife by nature, do not think,
To gratify thy lust for alien loves,
I would have helped thee hitherwards; but now
It is a mighty struggle for thy life,
And who saves life commits no injury.

PHÆDRA.

O close thy lips to such strange dreadful words,
And spare renewal of such shameful counsel!

NURSE.

Shameful perhaps, but better far for thee
Than all thy virtue; and this deed is nobler,
So be it save thy life, than any name
In which thou prid'st thyself, that brings thee death.

PHÆDRA.

Shameful thy words, but true; so, by the gods,
Say not thy say; my soul is crushed by love.
But if thou do make evil into good,
The snare I fain would flee from will entrap me.

NURSE.

Since so thou deem'st, the sin was sin in thought;
If not, listen, and grant a second favour.
I have at home philtres and soft love-spells;
Just now the thought flashed through me, one of these,
With no inducement to unrighteous action,

And no offence to conscience, might allay
This fever, so thou prove not still perverse.
Only there needs from him, from the beloved,
Some sign, a word, a fragment of his dress,
And from thyself the selfsame, like for like.
So shall the two together work one grace.

PHÆDRA.

Is it an ointment, or a drinking potion?

NURSE.

I know not : seek a cure, and not its nature.

PHÆDRA.

I fear thou wilt turn out too wise for me.

NURSE.

Thou fearest everything.   What alarm here?

PHÆDRA.

Lest thou say aught of this to Theseus' son.

NURSE.

Let be, dear child : I will set these things right;
Thou only help me, Cypris of the sea,
Thou work with me ! what else I meditate,
Enough to speak it to our friends within.

CHORUS.

Love, O Love, that, where thou willest,
From the loved one's eyes
Rain of soft desire distillest,
And the hearts of lovers fillest
With sweet auguries ;

Be no power for ill to me,
Break not up life's harmony.
Fiercest fires are fainter far,
Paler is the brightest star,
Than the darts that Love bids fly
From Aphrodité's armoury.
— Vainly by Alpheüs' water,
Vainly on each Pythian shrine,
Thick through Hellas steams the slaughter,
Bleed the lowing kine :
    If we fear not
    And revere not
Love the lord and Love the master,
    Love whose keys unlock at pleasure
    Aphrodité's fondest treasure,
Love who follows fast and faster
Everywhere on men below,
Death—where he will—or woe !
Thus Cypris wiled the fair Œchalian maid,
    A filly heedless of the yoke,
    Untouched by man, unwed :
Forth from her father's house she strayed,
    Like some fierce bacchanal she fled :
    Through blood, through smoke,
Through a bridal field of gore,
Alcmena's son the prize of victory bore.
Woe for such wedlock, woe !
City of sacred battlements,
    Thebes, and thou source of Dircé's silver flow,

Ye, had ye voice, could say with what intents
    Cypris moves subtly slow.
With cruel fate she hushed the life
Of Zeus' bride, the wedded wife
Of the thunder-bolt and the lightning-flame,
Whence Dionysus came.
She breathes upon all a wasting breath :
Like a bee where are sweets she hovereth.

PHÆDRA.

Silence, ye women ; I am lost, undone.

CHORUS.

Is aught amiss then, Phædra, in the house ?

PHÆDRA.

Hush ! I would catch the speech of those within.

CHORUS.

I am still ; sure this is prelude to some woe.

PHÆDRA.

Alas, alas ! ay me ! most pitiable,
Most pitiable for all my sufferings !

CHORUS.

What means this cry, what means this dole ?
Speak, speak ; say what, say where
The voice that storm-like stirs thy soul
And drives thee to despair ?

PHÆDRA.

Lost—I am lost.   Stand here beside these gates,
And listen to the clamour from within.

CHORUS.

Thou, thou stand there : for thee is meant
    The news from thence, alas !
Speak, speak, and say what new event
    Of ill has come to pass.

PHÆDRA.

The Amazon's son, Hippolytus, shouts aloud,
And heaps fiercest reproaches on the nurse.

CHORUS.

I hear a sound ; I hear it well ;
But whose and what I cannot tell.
A voice through the gates doth ring,
For thee, for thee is it echoing !

PHÆDRA.

He calls her by plain proof a procuress,
A traitress to her master's marriage-bed.

CHORUS.

Alas, alas ! they have betrayed thee,
Loved one, what can I do to aid thee?
For hidden things have come to light,
And thou art left in piteous plight.

PHÆDRA.

Ay me ! ay me !

CHORUS.

Thy friends have ruined thee.

PHÆDRA.

She has lost me by divulging all my sorrow,
Trying to cure it, kindly, but not wisely.

CHORUS.

What wilt thou do, poor helpless sufferer?

PHÆDRA.

I know not; saving this, forthwith to die:
Death is the sole help for such miseries.

HIPPOLYTUS.

O mother earth! O splendours of the sun!
What have I heard! what words unutterable!

NURSE.

Hush, hush, dear son, before thy voice is known.

HIPPOLYTUS.

I cannot hear such horrors, and keep silence.

NURSE.

Yes, by thy fair young arm and hand I pray thee.

HIPPOLYTUS.

Avaunt; let go my hand, touch not my robe.

NURSE.

By thy knees I pray thee bring me not to ruin.

HIPPOLYTUS.

Ruin?—thou say'st thou hast spoken nothing evil.

NURSE.

No; still not suited for the public ear.

HIPPOLYTUS.

If words are good, the more who hear the better.

NURSE.

Child, thou wilt never break thy plighted word?

HIPPOLYTUS.

If the lips swore, the heart abides unsworn.

NURSE.

Think what thou doest ; wilt thou destroy thy *friends ?*

HIPPOLYTUS.

I spurn them.—No wrongdoer is my friend.

NURSE.

Forgive them ; faults are natural to mortals.

HIPPOLYTUS.

O Zeus, why brought'st thou this adulterate metal,
This curse called woman into light of day ?
Were it thy will to breed the human race,
Thou shouldst not have made women the suppliers ;
But let such men as offered at thy fanes
Iron, or gold, or heavy store of brass,
Purchase the seed of children, each for each,
According to his value and his rank,
And people homes of freedom, without help
Of womankind. For see now, first of all,
When we would bring this curse into our house
We drain our homes of treasure : and 'tis clear
From this that woman is a monstrous evil,
For even her sire, that got and nurtured her,
Sends her away from home, and adds besides
A dowry, to be rid of such a plague.
While he who takes this mischief to his bosom
Exults, and heaps as on some foulest statue
Fair ornaments, and decks with finery :

Poor fool, exhausting his ancestral riches.
And here's his fate : either he gains alliance
With a good father, in requite for whom
He keeps a hateful wife ; or else the wife
Is good, the father profitless, and so
Ill-fortune presses on the heels of luck.
He is best off with neither, with a wife
Who sits at home in blank simplicity.
I hate a learned woman. None of mine
Be she who knows more than befits a woman.
'Tis in a clever soil that Cypris sows
The seeds of evil ; for a witless wife
By her scant wits is kept out of harm's way.
Therefore no servant should attend our women,
But monster mutes should bear them company,
So they might converse hold with none, and none
Might answer them in turn ; but now, alas,
Vile women in their homes plot villanies,
And hirelings carry their designs abroad.
Thus hast thou done, O wicked wicked head,
Coming to tempt me to unhallowed commerce
With my own father's wife ; coming with words
Which I will wash away with flowing water,
Purging my very ears. Could I be base,
I, who from only hearing of such crime,
Do almost doubt my chastity? Know this,
Mark well, my pious reverence saves thee, woman.
For hadst thou not, in an unguarded moment,
Entrapped me with an oath, I had not held

From telling the whole history to my sire.
Now from this roof, so long as from his land
Theseus abides, will I be absent too ;
And I will close my lips ; but when time comes
For turning hither in my father's track,
Then shall I see with what face thou wilt meet him,
Thou and thy mistress : then shall I discern
If thy effront'ry lasts thee like this sample.
My curse upon you.   Hate I you e'er so much,
No feast of hate can satisfy my greed,
Not if men cast my hatings in my teeth
As endless iteration,—seeing that ye
Some way or other endlessly are vile.
So, either some one teach them to be chaste,
Or let me trample on them endlessly.

CHORUS.

The fortunes of women are bad,
The fates of women are sad.
Is there any art we can learn,
Can any words be supplied,
That defeat may to victory turn,
And the knot of doom be untied ?

PHÆDRA.

O earth, O blessed sun,
The time of vengeance has begun !
Where can I wander from my fate?
How can I hide my wretched state ?
What god will help, what man will be my friend,

To give me counsel, or assistance lend
In godless deeds? alas, for this distress,
While this life lasts, there can be no redress !
Ay me, of women most unfortunate !

CHORUS.

Alas, 'tis done ; the nurse with all her arts
Has no success, but everything goes wrong.

PHÆDRA.

O wretch, O utter ruin to thy friends,
What hast thou done for me ? I pray that Zeus,
The author of my race, may blot thee out,
That root and branch he may annihilate thee,
And sear thee with his thunder.   Said I not,
Gave I not warning thou shouldst keep strict silence
On all the matter of my present sorrows ?
But thou wouldst not : therefore I cannot die—
There is no chance for it—with a fair name,
So must I look about for new devices.
For now this man, his mind sharp-edged with wrath,
Will tell in my disfavour all thy errors,
Will tell his sire, will tell the aged Pittheus,
Will fill with vilest rumours the whole land.
Perish both thou, and all like thee officious
In proffering to unwilling friends advice
Helpful in seeming, but in substance base.

NURSE.

Mistress, thou hast some cause to blame my fault,
Because the wound that eats into thy life

Passes all reasoning.   Yet, if thou wouldst hear,
I too have somewhat to reply to this.
I nursed thee, I do love thee ; and I sought
A cure for thy disease ; but what I sought
I found not : see now, if my plans had prospered,
I had been straightway held among the wise ;
For we weigh wisdom in the scales of chance.

PHÆDRA.

Is this then right,—will this make me amends,—
That first thou shouldst inflict a grievous hurt,
Then make it up by bandying arguments ?

NURSE.

We talk too much.   I know I was unwise ;
But, child, even now there may be help for thee.

PHÆDRA.

Have done with words.   There was no good before
In thy advice, and all thou didst was ill.
Get hence, begone ; plot plottings for thyself :
I will arrange my matters as I please.
But, noble daughters of Trœzenian birth,
Grant thus much to my prayers, and bury up
In silence all that ye have this day heard.

CHORUS.

We swear by Artemis, the child of Zeus,
Nought of thy woes shall be by us revealed.

PHÆDRA.

'Tis nobly said.   But after anxious search
I have but one help left for my disasters,

If I would have my children live in honour,
And aid myself in face of present failures;
For never, for the sake of life alone,
Will I cast shame upon my Cretan home,
Or come into the presence of my lord
Stained with the consciousness of evil deeds.

CHORUS.

Mean'st thou to work thyself some desperate harm?

PHÆDRA.

To die :—but how, I will myself devise.

CHORUS.

Speak not ill words.

PHÆDRA.

Give me not ill advice.
I shall give joy to Cypris, my destroyer,
In that I leave this life this very day,
And yield my vanquished self to love the victor.
Yet shall my death bring trouble on that other,
That he may know he shall not soar aloft
On my misfortune; he shall share my curse
Along with me, and learn too late forbearance.

CHORUS.

O that I were hid from sight
In the abysmal vaults of night,
And some god who saw me there,
Up among the flocks of air
Winged for flight would raise me high,
To join the sweet birds' company!

O'er the sea-waves would I soar
Foaming upon Adria's shore ;
O'er the champaign would I go
Where Eridanus doth flow,
And the sun-god's hapless daughters
Drop into his dark-blue waters
Amber tears, bright like the sun,
Wept for their lost Phaëthon.

Then far wandering over seas
I should reach the Hesperides,
All along whose blissful shore
Flowers and fruits bloom evermore :
Still they chaunt a solemn strain,
And the monarch of the main
Watches o'er the awful goal
Of the Atlas-shouldered pole,
And no mariner steers through
The silence of those waters blue,
Where are springs of nectar welling
Upwards towards Zeus's dwelling,
And the bounteous earth supplies
Ambrosia for the deities.

Cretan bark of snowy wing,
Thou from happy home didst bring
To a nuptial bed of woe
Her, my queen ; and thou didst go
O'er the billows lightly bounding,
O'er the great waves solemn-sounding.

Came the curse from Crete alone,
Or from sire and dame in one,
Under Athens haughty-crested
Fraught with ill the shallop rested,
To Munychia's rugged ground
Twisted cable ends were bound
All for ill; and on dry land
For ill the voyagers did stand.

Quickly then no pure desire
Aphrodité did inspire,
And her heart was broken, broken
By this fell disease unspoken:
So, with sorrow overborne,
In her bridal room forlorn,
Round about her neck of snow
She the halter-noose will throw,
For she fears this hateful power,
And, with fair fame for her dower,
Fain she would from love be free,—
Love that is but misery.

MESSENGER.

What ho!
Within there; run for help; shout, all of ye
Our lady, Theseus' wife, hangs in the noose.

CHORUS.

Alas, then, all is over; and our queen
Is queen no more, held fastly in the halter!

MESSENGER.

Make haste. Not one of ye to bring a knife
Two-edged, to sever from her neck the knot?

SEMI-CHORUS I.

What must we do, friends? should we go within,
And free the queen out of the tight-drawn noose?

SEMI-CHORUS II.

Stay. Why come not the young men of the household?
Much meddling does not make life all the safer.

MESSENGER.

Straighten her limbs; lay out her hapless corpse.
Truly a woful mistress for our master.

CHORUS.

She is dead, then, as I hear, unhappy lady!
Already as a corpse they lay her out.

THESEUS.

Know ye what means this cry within the house,
Good women?—for there comes a mournful sound
Of household voices; and none take the pains
To hail me travelled from the oracle,
To ope the door or bid a kindly welcome.
Has aught, then, happened to the aged Pittheus?
He has gone very far in life; but still
'Twere a sad grief to see my home without him.

CHORUS.

Theseus, this fortune aims not at the aged;
The young, the young are dead, and claim thy sorrow.

THESEUS.

Alas, one of my children robbed of life?

CHORUS.

They live; their mother has died dismally.

THESEUS.

Dead, say'st thou? My wife dead? Say when, say
how.

CHORUS.

She tied herself fast to the noosèd halter.

THESEUS.

Had grief, then, palsied her, or what mischance?

CHORUS.

We know no more: we are but just arrived
In time to sorrow, Theseus, for thy sorrows.

THESEUS.

Ay me!—for what, then, is my forehead wreathed
With woven garlands, since the oracle
Brings me but woe? What ho there, slaves within,
Unbar the doors, undo the fastenings,
That I may look upon my wife's sad end,
And see the death that is as death to me.

CHORUS.

Alas for thy sorrows! alas for thy fate!
The suffering undergone,
The sad deed thou hast done,
Would make the whole house desolate.
O the will unbending!
O the forceful ending!

O the hand that with unholy grasp
To thy throat the fatal rope did clasp !
Tell me, tell what power of might
Hath quenched thy life in endless night ?

THESEUS.

Pity me also, most unfortunate !
Mine are the greatest sufferings.   O fate,
Thou weighest heavy on my house and me,—
A plague-spot from some vengeful deity,
That no one looked for,—to such ruin growing
That life's not worth the living ; for I see
An ocean wide of ills so overflowing
That I can never hope to swim to land,
Nor stem the wave of such calamity.
Can any words, can any tongue express
The heavy, heavy weight of thy distress ?
For, like a bird, thou hast escaped my hand,
And winged thy sudden flight far, far away,
To gloomy Hades.   O this luckless day !
To some far-distant source this woe I trace ;
For sins of sires oppress their latest race.

CHORUS.

Not to thee only, king, is sent this sorrow ;
Full many another mourns a precious wife.

THESEUS.

O were I sunk in subterraneous gloom !
That everlasting darkness were my doom,
Now I have lost thy sweet society !

Killing thyself, thou hast more than killed me.
Where shall I hear how such death-bearing fate
Pierced thy sad heart? who will the tale relate?
Or do my palace-roofs shelter in vain
A hireling troop? I weep, I weep thy pain,
No heart could bear, no tongue could say
The sorrows I have seen to-day.
In ruin I am left,
My children are bereft,
My house is left unto me desolate.

CHORUS.

Dearest lady, thou art gone,
Best the sun e'er looked upon,
Or the moon that walks the night
Girt with many a starry light.

Alas, poor lord, what ills this house doth know!
O, when I think upon thy present woe,
Down from my eyes in streams the hot tears pour;
But yet I shudder most at that which is in store.

THESEUS.

O look, O look, what means this writing-tablet?
See, it is fastened to her tender hand,
And, of a surety, it hath news for me.
She writes, perhaps, some fond petitionings
About her children or our wedding-bond.—
Take heart, poor shade; there is no living woman
Shall reign in Theseus' halls, or share his bed.—-

And yet the impress of her golden seal
(Her that is now no more) looks like a welcome.
Haste, haste, undo the sealèd fastenings,
And let me read what she would say to me.

CHORUS.

Alas, alas, the god heaps woe on woe,
    One on another comes in dread succession !
Fain would I every joy in life forego,
    If of my friends such fates must hold possession.
For now I look on this whole family
    As things that are not, not as things that are.
    If it may be, ye powers, in pity spare
This house, and listen to my suppliant cry.
For somehow, like an augur, I descry
Far off the bodings of calamity.

THESEUS.

O what a sorrow added to my sorrows,
Unbearable, unspeakable : woe's me !

CHORUS.

What, what ?   O speak, if I may share the news.

THESEUS.

This writing has a voice, a shriek
To shriek a tale most damnable ; where can I seek
A hiding-place from such hell-host ?
O, I am lost, lost, lost !
O what a wretched woe these letters speak !
What wretched eyes behold !

CHORUS.

Thy words move in the van of many woes.

THESEUS.

This hellish wrong I will no longer keep
Imprisoned by my lips ; it shall not sleep,
In that there is no help for it, untold.
O city, listen to me,—I say, O city,—
Hippolytus has dared to assail my bed,
Regardless of the holy eye of Zeus.
But, father mine, Poseidon of the sea,
Take one of those three wishes that erewhile
Thou gavest me ; and kill this son of mine,
And, so thou gav'st them me not bootlessly,
Let not this day go by and leave him living.

CHORUS.

King, by the gods, pray back that prayer again.
Trust me, in time thou wilt find out thy error.

THESEUS.

It cannot be.   Also from this my land
I will expel him ; so that of two fates,
By one or other he must be o'erwhelmed.
Either Poseidon, honouring my curse,
To Hades will dismiss his lifeless body,
Or, exiled from this land, he shall exhaust
On alien soil a wretched wandering life.

CHORUS.

Look, on the instant comes into thy presence
Hippolytus, thy son.   O pray thee, king,

Relax thy ill-spent wrath, and of thy house
Bethink thee, what may best be done for it.

HIPPOLYTUS.

Father, I heard the clamour of thy voice,
And hasten to thy presence; but of that
Which moves thee to such mourning knowing nought,
Fain would I hear it from thyself.   O mercy!
What do I see?   Father, is this thy wife,—
A corpse?—this is most wonderful of wonders.
She whom I lately left,—she who beheld
But a few moments past the light of day!
What fate befel her? how came she to perish?
O father, I am anxious for thy words.
Why art thou silent? silence helps not grief.
The heart that longs for all intelligence
Hungers the more to share in news of sorrow;
And thou, my father, dost not right to hide
Thy woe from friends, — from something more than
        friends.

THESEUS.

O men that walk in paths of endless error,
What boot your thousand arts, your sciences,
The compass of invention, if one thing,
One little thing, ye know not, hunt not out,
How to teach sense to those that have it not?

HIPPOLYTUS.

In faith, he were a sage of passing wit
That could turn idiots into reasoning men,

But,—for it never was thy custom, father,
In time of need to play with quibbling words,—
I fear thy tongue is overborne by sorrow.

THESEUS.

Yes, we should have some certain evidence,
Some clear discrimination of our friends,
To tell us who is false and who is true.
Men should have two tongues all; one for the truth,
And one to suit the time : so should the false,
That plotted lies, be by the true convicted,
And we ourselves be rid of all deception.

HIPPOLYTUS.

If some maligning fiend has stol'n thy ear,
Then must I suffer from no fault of mine ;
I am struck dumb ; thy words are terrible,
Wild wandering words, without a show of reason.

THESEUS.

O, whither will this human nature tend ?
Shall nothing limit its audacity,
Its daring know no bounds ? for if it grow
With increase of our race commensurate,
So that the son be baser than his sire,
And each descendant add a thousandfold
To sins of those before him, then, in faith,
The gods must add another earth to this,
That there be room for traitors and for knaves.
Look here now on this man, sprung from my loins ;
He has disgraced my bed : the dead herself

Proves him most clearly vilest of the vile.
Yet showest thou thy face before thy father,
After attempt of such a heinous crime.
Thou keepest company with gods, forsooth,
As better than thy fellows? thou art chaste,
And spotless?—let me not believe thy vaunts,
And charge the gods with ignorance of evil.
Boast if thou wilt, then; trick men in thy eating;
Choose bloodless food; take Orpheus for thy king;
Dance, shout i' the orgies; hold in much esteem
A misty fog of scribblings;—thou art caught,
Thou art caught in the act; and thee, and such as thee,
I bid all men stand far from; for they hunt,
They compass round their prey with pious phrases,
Devising villanous plots. Thy prey is dead;
She is dead. Think'st thou her death will make thee
    safe?
O wretch, it is thy very certain ruin.
What oaths, what words can overbear this witness,
And of this charge acquit thee? Wilt thou say
She hated thee? that thou, a bastard child,
Wast odious to my seed legitimate?
Thou mak'st her in the merchandise of life
But a poor trader, if for hate of thee
She gave up all that was most dear to her.
Thou say'st perchance that such foolhardy passion
Is foreign to a man, albeit it thrives
A part of woman's nature; yet I know,
When Cypris stirs the springtide of the heart,

E

Youths are no more secure than womankind,—
Their sex too gives them shelter.　Now away!
Why wrestle I with sophisms of thine?
She who lies dead is plainest evidence.
Begone thou from this land in instant flight,
And rest not under Athens' god-built towers,
Nor on the outskirts of what land soe'er
My arms compel; no, if I suffered this,
And yielded to it, let that Isthmus thief,
That Sinis, never bear me witness more
I killed him, but gave tongue to empty vaunts;
Nor those Scironides, sea-skirting rocks,
Confess that I fell heavy on the wicked.

CHORUS.

I cannot say that any man is happy;
All that seemed good at first is changed to evil.

HIPPOLYTUS.

Father, thy wrath, the fixture of thy mind,
Is fearful; yet could one unfold this tale,
That on the face of it thou readest right,
There were no fair ground for accusing me.
I am not gifted to address a crowd,
But in the presence of a few, my equals,
My speech is counted wise: and this is reason;
For they whose talk is nothing to the wise,
Their words go down like music with the mob.
Yet must I, in the face of present fates,
Unlock my tongue; and I will launch my speech

Where thou assail'dst me first, and struck me down,
Whelmed, as thou thought'st, and powerless to reply.
Seest thou this light of day? seest thou this earth?
There lives no man who shares this light, this earth,
Deny it as thou wilt, more chaste than me.
For I have learned first to revere the gods,
Next to have friends that tempt not godlessness,
But men who shrink from giving place to evil,
And back not up wrongdoers in their wrong.
I am no scoffer at my comrades, father;
Absent or present to my friends the same.
And of one thing thou now wouldst fix on me
I am spotless; even to this very moment
There has no love-stain rested on my life,
Nor know I of love's practice, save from talk
That I have heard, and pictures I have seen,
Which I was never forward to behold,
Seeing that I have kept a virgin heart.
Yet, if my chastity obtains no credence—
Haply it does not—thou at least must show
When and by what means it became corrupted.
Did, then, this form so far surpass in beauty
All other women? or did I expect
To get thy wife, thy palace, and a dowry?
I were a fool then, with no gleam of sense.
But power is sweet?—far from it to the wise,
Save where delight of sovereignty has spoiled
The better judgment: where I would be first
Is in the Hellene games; but in the state

Hold second place, among my chosen friends
Sharing good fortune, that in life like this
May be attained, while absence of all peril
Makes us more happy far than joys of empire.
I have one thing else to say; the rest is said.
Had I one witness like unto myself,
And could she, to the light of day restored,
Abide the contest, then wouldst thou discern
Who was the wicked one ; but now I swear
By Zeus the inviolable and by mother Earth,
I never touched thy wife, nor wished, nor dreamed
Such thing.   O, may I die in infamy,
Nameless, without a city or a home,
A roaming fugitive from land to land,
And let not sea or earth receive my bones
When I am dead, if I have acted basely.
Now, if she took her life in sudden terror,
I know not.   I am sealed from saying more.
She is held chaste that had no chastity,
And I that have it make poor profit by it.

CHORUS.

Thou hast made full rebutment of this charge,
Calling the gods to witness, no slight warrant.

THESEUS.

Have we not here some cheat, some conjuror,
That trusts, after dishonouring his father,
To win his heart back with smooth blandishments?

HIPPOLYTUS.

Father, I am amazed at thee in this :
For hadst thou been my son, and I thy father,
I would have slain thee, and not exiled thee,
If thou hadst ventured to attempt my wife.

THESEUS.

Right worthy of thee this ! thou diest not so.
Not at thy own arranging ; for swift death
Is punishment too light for wicked men.
Thou, wandering far from thine own fatherland,
On alien soil shalt wearily drag out
A bitter life ; this is the wage of sin.

HIPPOLYTUS.

Alas, what mean'st thou ? wilt not wait awhile
Till time shall bring to light my innocence ?
Wilt drive me on the instant from the land ?

THESEUS.

Aye, and beyond the sea, and, if I could,
Beyond the threshold of this universe,
With such abhorrence do I look upon thee.

HIPPOLYTUS.

And wilt thou, then, regard no oath, no pledge ?
And wilt thou question no diviner's art,
But cast me from the land untried, unjudged ?

THESEUS.

This letter—this—from no diviner's hand,
Comes and accuses thee ; and I believe it.

But for the birds that flit over my head,
I bid them and their auguries good-day.

HIPPOLYTUS.

Ye gods, why do I not unloose my tongue,—
I, who must perish through my reverence
And worship of you ?   Yet it cannot be.
I could not whom I would the more convince,
And for no good should break the vow I vowed.

THESEUS.

O heavens, this piety of thine will kill me !
Wilt thou not get thee gone out of the land ?

HIPPOLYTUS.

And whither shall I turn, ay me ! what friend
Will harbour me, an exile on such charge ?

THESEUS.

Whoever takes delight to entertain
Corrupters of men's wives, or aids in crime.

HIPPOLYTUS.

This cuts me to the heart ; this comes nigh weeping,
To appear base to others and to thee.

THESEUS.

Then was the time for moans and presagings,
When thou didst dare insult thy father's wife.

HIPPOLYTUS.

O roof, would thou hadst voice to speak for me,
And witness whether villain be my name !

THESEUS.

Thou fliest to dumb witnesses ?—but know
It is not words, but deeds, that stamp thee villain.

HIPPOLYTUS.

Ah, could I take another shape, and stand
And see myself,—how should I weep my woes !

THESEUS.

Thou art much more wont, like many holy men,
To love thyself than to respect thy parents.

HIPPOLYTUS.

O hapless mother ! O unhappy offspring !
May never a one of my friends be base-born !

THESEUS.

Will ye not drag him, slaves ?—did ye not hear
That long ago I told him to be gone ?

HIPPOLYTUS.

If one of them but touch me, he shall rue it :
Drive me out thou thyself, if such thy will.

THESEUS.

And so I will, if thou obeyest me not ;
There is no place for pity in my heart.

HIPPOLYTUS.

It seems my doom is fixed, then. Woe is me !
I know it now ; I know not what to say.
O best-beloved of the Olympian host,
My partner, my companion in the chase,
O Artemis, I am condemned to fly

From glorious Athens. Farewell, then, O city;
Farewell, Erechtheus' land; and thou, farewell,
Thou shore of Trœzen, where all joys abound
That make a young life happy,—O, farewell.
This is the last word I shall speak to thee;
This is the last time I shall look on thee.
Come, then, my comrades, flower of the land,
Bid me god-speed, and give me friendly escort;
For never will ye see a purer man,
Though I am other in my father's eyes.

CHORUS.

Oft, when I think what care the gods bestow,
   I cease from grieving as I grieved before;
Till sight of sins and sorrows here below
   Makes judgment totter, and hope die once more.
      For this and that thing changes,
      And human life still ranges
Through wildering maze of varied joy and woe.
O, would some god in answer to my prayer
   Grant me a share of fortune and success;
A name not passing great nor falsely fair;
   A quiet heart unfurrowed by distress!
      Then should I wile away
      From day to happy day
A long unbroken life of blissfulness.
Now am I ill at ease; my hopes are spent;
   For I have seen our Athens' brightest star
Dimmed by a father's wrath; have seen him sent
   Alone on alien soil to wander far.

O rippled sands upon my country's shore,
   O thick oak-coppice on the mountain grey,
Where with Dictynna thou didst chase the boar,
   And urge thy fleet hounds on her destined prey ;
No more shalt thou see yoked thy Adrian steeds,
Or curb their flying course round Limna's meads ;
The muse that slept not on the tuneful strings,
Through the old halls shall cease her echoings ;
In the lush grass what time she lays her head,
Latona's child must rest ungarlanded ;
And all the rival maids that sighed for thee
Must mourn unwedded thy calamity.
Yet in thy luckless luck will I have share ;
   My tears shall weep thy pain.
Alas, O hapless mother that didst bear
   Child-bearing pangs in vain !
O gods, I am wroth with ye ; O sweet-linked band
   Of Graces, wherefore send this innocent
Far from his father's land,
   Far from his home to dreary banishment?
And look, I do behold one of his servants
Hasting with downcast eyes towards the palace.

SECOND MESSENGER.

Where shall I find the monarch of this land,
King Theseus ? If ye know, good women, show me.
Perhaps he is within the palace walls.

CHORUS.

This is the king himself who issues forth.

SECOND MESSENGER.

Theseus, I bring a message of great burden
To thee and all the citizens who dwell
In Athens or by Trœzen's extreme shore.

THESEUS.

What now?   Has any fresh calamity
Fall'n unawares on the twin neighbour cities?

SECOND MESSENGER.

To speak it short—Hippolytus is no more;
Still seeing the light, but on the verge of death.

THESEUS.

Death at whose hands? whose wrath has he in-
          curred?
Whose wife has he assaulted, like his father's?

SECOND MESSENGER.

The wheels of his own chariot are his death—
They, and the prayers that to thy sea-king sire
Thine own lips uttered against thine own son.

THESEUS.

O gods!—O thou Poseidon, without doubt
Thou hast proved thyself my father, having heard
My curse, and answered it.
                    Thou now, speak out
The manner of his death, and by what means
The trap of justice fell on him that shamed me.

SECOND MESSENGER.

We by the margin of the wave-washed shore
Were smoothing out with combs our coursers' manes
In sore distress : because a message came
Hippolytus should no more rest his foot
Upon the soil, having been doomed by thee
To hopeless exile ; and anon himself
Came laden with the selfsame dirge of tears,
And all along the shore a myriad host
Of friends and comrades followed in his track.
But when the wailing ceased, and he found tongue—
" Why am I thus distraught ? my father's words
Must be obeyed," he said ; " therefore, ye slaves,
Harness my steeds, and yoke them to my car ;
For now this city is no more for me"—
Then straightway every man bestirred himself,
And, almost ere his tongue could speak his will,
The bridled steeds were ready for our lord.
He from the chariot-rail unloosed the reins,
Took them, and on the foot-board set his feet ;
And first with outspread hands the gods invoked :
" Zeus, let me die the death, if I be base ;
But whether dead, or whether I yet see
The blessed light, O may my father know
How he has wronged me for no wrong of mine !"
So saying, with the whip he urged his steeds,
And all the throng that hung about his reins
Followed our lord along the road direct
To Argos through the Epidaurian land.

But when we came unto a barren tract,
Beyond the frontier of this realm, a shore
That stretches down to the Saronic sea,
There came a sound, as if some bolt from Zeus
Made thunder from the bowels of the earth,
A heavy hollow boom, hideous to hear ;
At which the coursers lifted up their heads
To heaven, and pricked their ears ; and as for us,
A sudden fear fell on our youthful hearts,
Whence came this awful voice ; till with fixed gaze
Watching the sea-beat ridges, we beheld
A mighty billow lifted to the skies,
That robbed my sight of the Scironian rocks,
And shrouded all the Isthmus, and the peak
Of Æsculapius, and with seething gurge
And white environment of hissing foam
Gasped by the raging water, shoreward moved,
Where by the sea-beach stood the four-horsed car.
And with the billow, at the third great sweep
Of mountain-surge, the sea gave up a bull,
Monster of aspect fierce, whose bellowings
Filled all the earth, that echoed back the roar
In tones that made us shudder ; and who saw,
Saw what appeared too awful to be seen.
But, when the steeds were seized with sudden fright,
Our lord, in all their ways long conversant,
Grasped at the reins, and throwing back his weight,
Pulled hard, as pulls a sailor at the oar ;
They with set jaws gripping the tempered bits,

Whirl along heedless of the master's hand,
And of the reins, and of the carven car ;
And if at times he steered them towards smooth
     ground,
Loomed in their front the bull, and drove them back,
A frenzied team ; but when towards the cliffs
They swept in madness, he kept close beside
In silence, striding by the chariot-wheels,
Till 'gainst a rugged crag he jammed the axle,
And tripped the chariot up, and overturned it.
Then all was whelmed in ruin ; the wheel-naves
Were tost above the wheels, and from the axles
The linchpins started.   He, poor helpless one,
Meshed in the tangled harness, and held fast
In bonds indissoluble, is dragged along.
His loved head dashed against the cruel rocks,
His flesh all torn, his shrieks most pitiful,
" O, stand," he cries, " ye that have drawn your food
Out of my mangers,—drag me not to death.
Alas, alas, my father's fatal curse !
Who will come save a man spotless of wrong ?"
And many wished, but our too tardy steps
Left us far from him, who, I know not how,
Slipped from the harness fetterings, and fell,
With little breath of life yet left in him.
But of the horses we saw nothing more,
Nor the thrice-cursed monster of a bull,
That vanished 'mong the rocks, I know not where.
King, I am but a slave about thy palace,

Yet to one thing I never will give credence,
That this thy son has done a deed of baseness,
Not should the whole of womankind go hang,
And score the pines of Ida with their letters,
Because I know—I know that he is noble.

CHORUS.

Alas, the latest woes are all fulfilled!
There is no help from fate and destiny.

THESEUS.

Because I hate him who has met this doom,
The story gives me pleasure ; but because
I reverence the gods, and even this man,
Seeing he is sprung from me, I cannot joy
At what I hear, nor yet can I be wroth.

SECOND MESSENGER.

Must we convey him here?—what shall we do
For the poor youth to satisfy thy will?
Consider ;—thou wilt not, could I advise,
Show cruelty to thy unhappy son.

THESEUS.

Carry him here, that I may see before me
Him who denies having defiled my bed,
And prove his guilt, and make his fate confute him.

CHORUS.

O Cypris, thou canst move
   Hearts that no softness know,
The hearts of gods above,
   The hearts of men below.

And Love with plumage gay
Flashes his lightning way,
And flits along the earth with thee,
And hovers o'er the sounding sea.
When 'gainst a frenzied heart
Love sets him in array,
He wings a golden dart,
And wins the heart away :
Dogs on the mountains feel him,
The ocean-broods reveal him ;
Whate'er the sun beholds,
Whate'er his bright beams warm,
Whate'er the earth enfolds,
Confess the wizard's charm :
Men know it too ; and, Cypris, all things own
Thy might, and hail thee as their queen alone.

ARTEMIS.

I summon thee, O noble son of Ægeus,
To listen to my words ; and I who speak
Am Artemis, Latona's virgin daughter.
    This is poor matter, Theseus, for content ;
Thou hast unjustly robbed thy son of life,
Trusting the lying letters of thy wife,
And without proofs hast worked thy sad intent.
Thou art fall'n into a very evident doom :
Why dost not haste deep in the infernal gloom
To hide thy face for shame ? or else to change
Into a bird, and soar through regions strange

To all this sorrow ?—for among just men
Thou never canst have part or lot again.
   Now listen, Theseus, to the history
Of thy disasters ; I am powerless
To cut them short, yet do I grieve for thee.
This will I do : I will make clear to all
Thy son's integrity, that he may die
In honour, and thy wife's frenzied desire,
And, in some fashion too, her nobleness ;
For, goaded on by her of all above
Most hateful to our virgin-happy hearts,
She yearned after thy son ; and when she tried
By exercise of will to vanquish Cypris,
She fell, unwilling, by her nurse's craft,
Who under covert of an oath revealed
This sickness to thy son. He, in all troth,
Seconded not her pleadings ; and again,
When foully wronged by thee, flung not away
His plighted word, being a righteous man.
And she, in fear of judgment that might follow,
Wrote lying writings, and destroyed thy son
By frauds that nathless thou didst take as truths.

THESEUS.

Alas, alas !

ARTEMIS.

Has this a fang to pierce thee ? yet be still,
And listen more, that thou mayst sorrow more.
Thou know'st thy father gave to thee three wishes,

Separate and sure. The first, meet for a foe,
Most wickedly thou hurledst at thy son.
Which, in good faith towards thee, thy sea-king sire
Granted, and since he promised, granted right.
Yet thou art hateful in his eyes and mine;
For neither didst thou stay for confirmation,
Nor answer of the seers, nor test nor proof,
Nor gavest time, ever so little time,
As was thy duty, but with headlong haste
Didst hurl the curse, and doom thy son to die.

THESEUS.

Mistress, would I were dead !

ARTEMIS.

Awful thy sin ;
Yet even for thee there may be room for pardon.
For Cypris willed that these things should be so,
To glut her rage ; and this with gods is law,
That none against another's will resists,
Or offers hindrance, but we stand aloof.
Else, be assured, had not the fear of Zeus
Deterred me, I had not so sunk in shame
As to let die the dearest unto me
Of mortal men ; but for this sin of thine,
Ignorance first of all frees thee of soil.
Next thy dead wife, with whom have likewise died
The only proofs that could have well convinced thee.
Chiefly on thee these sorrows have outbroken ;
My share is grief : for gods take not delight

F

When good men die ; but as for evil-doers,
We root them up, their children, and their homes.

CHORUS.

He is coming—O sight forlorn !—
His tender flesh all torn,
His fair locks fouled with gore.
O house, thou art troubled sore ;
For sorrow and sorrow, twin-born,
The gods for its fate have given ;
And fulfilled is the doom of heaven.

HIPPOLYTUS.

Pity me, pity me !
By a wicked decree
From the lips of a sire unjust,
Shattered, laid low in the dust.
It is done ; I shall soon be dead ;
Sharp pains strike through my head,
Quick spasms dart through my brain.
Stay, stay ;
Let me rest my faint limbs again.
O cursèd chariot-coursers, fed
By me, from my hands nourishèd,
Ye have killed me, ye have rent my life away.
O gently, by the gods I pray,
Touch my torn flesh, good slaves. Who is he
                    doth stand
Beside me, close at my right hand ?
Lift all together, raise up with care

Me the ill-fated,
Mistakenly hated,
O Zeus, canst thou see and forbear ?
I the holy, the god-fearing,
A too-evident death am nearing ;
I, above all others chaste,
Root and branch must be cut off ;
And the world may justly scoff
At my pious labours' waste.
Ah ! alas ! alas ! again
Through me, through me strikes the pain.
O set me down, O let me be,
And Death the healer come to me.
Kill, kill me, end my misery, I pray :
O for a two-edged blade to sweep
The very shreds of flesh away,
And cradle me in endless sleep !
O wretched prayer for a sire to pray !

    From kith and kin,
    Blood-stained and men of sin,
    From our sires of long ago,
    Sprang this woe,
On me accomplished with no more delay.
Yet why on me ? why fell it on me,
The guiltless of all infamy ?
Alas ! what shall I say ?
How from this cruel pain can I get free ?
Welcome, dim Hades ; welcome, night of doom :
And let me sink to sleep amid the gloom.

ARTEMIS.

Poor sufferer, thou art linked to a sad fate ;
Thy noble heart hath been thy sad undoing.

HIPPOLYTUS.

O breath of heavenly savour! even in pain
I know thee, and a load is off my heart.
She is here, the goddess Artemis is here.

ARTEMIS.

Poor soul, she is ; dearest of powers to thee.

HIPPOLYTUS.

O mistress, seest thou my wretched state ?

ARTEMIS.

I see it ; but I may not shed a tear.

HIPPOLYTUS.

Thou hast no more a huntsman or a servant.

ARTEMIS.

No more.   Thou whom I love art overthrown.

HIPPOLYTUS.

Nor charioteer, nor guardian of thy statues.

ARTEMIS.

Because that wicked Cypris so has planned it.

HIPPOLYTUS.

Ah, now I see the power that has destroyed me.

ARTEMIS.

Grieved by neglect, and hating chastity,

HIPPOLYTUS.

I see it : three of us has Cypris wrecked.

ARTEMIS.

Thy sire, thyself, thirdly thy father's wife.

HIPPOLYTUS.

That too I weep for, for my father's sorrows.

ARTEMIS.

He was beguilèd by immortal wiles.

HIPPOLYTUS.

O father, thou hast fallen on evil fates.

THESEUS.

I am lost, my son ; life is no joy to me.

HIPPOLYTUS.

For thee I sorrow more than for myself.

THESEUS.

O son, that I were in thy place a corpse !

HIPPOLYTUS.

O bitter gifts thy sire Poseidon gave thee !

THESEUS.

Would that such words had never passed my lips !

HIPPOLYTUS.

What matter? such thy rage, thou wouldst have killed
me.

THESEUS.

The gods had stolen away my better mind.

HIPPOLYTUS.

Surely the gods hold mortals as a curse.

ARTEMIS.

Enough; let be.   Not without due requite
Shall Cypris launch her fury at thy life,
And sink thee in the gloom because thy heart
Is pure, and thou art set on piety.
For with my own hand I will seek out one
Dearer to her than any mortal man,
And he shall die by this unerring bow.
But thee, poor sufferer, I will recompense
With highest honours in this town of Trœzen;
For girls unwed, before their marriage-day,
Shall offer their shorn tresses at thy shrine,
And dower thee through long ages with rich tears;
And many a maid shall raise the tuneful hymn
In praise of thee, and ne'er shall Phædra's love
Perish in silence and be left unsung.
Now, son of aged Ægeus, take thy son,
Draw him towards thee, fold him in thy arms.
His fate is not thy will; and when the gods
Urge mortals on, no wonder mortals err.

And, lov'd Hippolytus, I do exhort thee
Look not with any hate upon thy father;
For fate has willed thy death.   And now farewell;
I may not look upon the dead ; my sight
May not be sickened by death-agonies.
And I behold thee nearing to the end.

HIPPOLYTUS.

Thou, too, depart in peace, O blessed maid!
Farewell; and mayst thou with light heart forget
Our long companionship! See, at thy hest,
As in old days I hearkened to thy words,
So now I end all quarrel with my father.
Ay me! my eyes are growing dim.   Come, father,
Take me, and straighten out my limbs for rest.

THESEUS.

My son! what dost thou to thy hapless father?

HIPPOLYTUS.

I die.   I see the very gates of Hades.

THESEUS.

Wilt thou leave me unpurged of all my sin?

HIPPOLYTUS.

O no; because I free thee of my murder.

THESEUS.

What? dost thou take the load of blood from off
    me?

HIPPOLYTUS.

Queen of the bow, be witness, Artemis!

THESEUS.

Thou art truly noble, lov'd one, towards thy father.

HIPPOLYTUS.

Now, father dear, farewell, a long farewell!

THESEUS.

O what a pure and godlike heart is thine!

HIPPOLYTUS.

Pray thou mayst have true children such as me.

THESEUS.

Leave me not yet, my son; bear up in patience.

HIPPOLYTUS.

Patience is past with me; my hour has come.
Father, make speed to cover up my face.

THESEUS.

O realm of Athens, Pallas' sacred soil,
What a great heart we are robbed of! woe is me!
I have small reason to forget thee, Cypris.

CHORUS.

Upon all in the city alike
This sudden sorrow will strike.

There will be much shedding of tears.
When evil assails the great
Many bewail his fate;
   Grief for him grows with the years.

SELECT IDYLS OF THEOCRITUS.

IDYL I.

Thyrsis.

THYRSIS.

Soft sighs a breath of whispered melody
From yonder pine beside the fountain-heads,
And, herdsman, sweet thy pipe; thine be the prize
Next after Pan; if his a hornèd goat,
A she-goat shall be thine; and if he choose
A she-goat for his guerdon, then a kid
Falls to thy lot; and meat of kid is good
Till she be grown to milking.

HERDSMAN.

     Sweeter far
Thy music, shepherd, than the plashing fall
Of rivulets from yonder topmost rocks.
Sure, if the Muses choose a fleecy gift,
A tender nursling lamb be thy reward;
And if a lamb, so please they, be for them,
Thou afterward shalt lead a sheep away.

THYRSIS.

Wilt thou sit here, by the Nymphs, wilt sit and pipe
Beside this rising hill in tamarisk shade?
And I will let my goats go browse around.

HERDSMAN.

We must not, shepherd, at the noon-tide hour
We must not, dare not pipe for fear of Pan.
For then he rests from labours of the chase,
And he is fierce, and very bitter wrath
Sits ever on his nostril. But, come now,—
For, Thyrsis, thou canst sing of Daphnis' griefs,
And thou hast touched the heights of rural song,—
Sit we beneath yon elm, hard by the shrine
Of old Priapus and the water-nymphs,
Where shepherds use to sit, and where are oaks.
And so thou singest as once thou sang'st before,
In strife with Chromis who hailed from Libya,
I will give thee a goat, a mother of twins,
With threefold store of milk for those two kids,
The filling of two pails; and I will give
A deep two-handled goblet, lined within
With pliant wax, quite new, fresh from the chisel;
And round its topmost margin ivy twines
Sprinkled with helichryse, whose crocus-bloom
Is clasped by loving tendrils; and inside
Is wrought a woman of divinest shape,
In grace of robe and snood, and long-haired men
From one to other toss the strife of words,

Question and answer; but it moves not *her:*
For now she looks at this one with a smile,
And now her thoughts turn otherwhere; but they
With eyes love-rolling toil and strive in vain.
And there is an old fisher, and beside
A rugged rock, whereon he braces him
To hold his net for a cast, as fits a man
Of mighty labour; so that one would say
He fished with every muscle; round his neck
The veins swell up; and though his head is gray,
His strength seems like a boy's. And not far off
The old seafarer droops a blooming vine,
Heavy with red ripe grapes. A little boy
Sits on a wall and guards them. Round him come
Two foxes, one among the vineyard-lines
Creeps stealthy, pillaging the dainty fruit;
The other, plotting every sort of wile
Against his knapsack, vows not to desert
The lad before he make him breakfastless;
Who all the while weaves a fair wicker-trap
To catch cicadas in an osier mesh;
And cares not for his knapsack or his fruit,
So much his work delights him. And all round
The moist acanthus floats about the cup,
Æolian in workmanship, a wonder
To take away thy breath. For this I gave
A she-goat to a man from Calydon,
A sailor, and a mighty white-milk cheese,
Fair price,—nor has it ever touched my lips,

But there it lies unstained,—which now to thee
With much content I offer for thy joy,
So thou be fain to sing to me that song
I long for.   Think not I am envious,
But sing, good friend; thy music will not sound
When Hades holds thee in forgetfulness.

THYRSIS.

Lead, Muses, lead our rural melody.
Thyrsis is here, from Ætna's slopes; the voice
Of Thyrsis speaks.   Where, Muses, had ye fled;
Where were ye, nymphs, when Daphnis died away?
In some fair Tempé, where Peneüs rolls,
Or Pindus rises; for ye did not haunt
The great waves of Anapus, nor the peak
Of Ætna, neither Acis' holy stream.

Lead, Muses, lead our rural melody.
Him mourned the lynxes, him the wild wolves mourned,
The lion in the thicket wept his death.

Lead, Muses, lead our rural melody.
Before his feet much oxen, many bulls,
And many a cow and heifer stood and wailed.

Lead, Muses, lead our rural melody.
Came Hermes from the mountain first of all,
And whispered, " Daphnis, who has worked thee this?
For whom, O dear one, dost thou burn with love?"

Lead, Muses, lead our rural melody.
Came round him herdsmen, shepherds, goatherds came,

And questioned his ill-fortune. Came Priapus,
And said, " Poor Daphnis, why dost waste away ?
Lo she, the maid herself, with wandering feet
By every fountain, and through every copse,
(Lead, Muses, lead our rural melody.)
Pursues in search : sure thou art slow to love,
And all distraught. A herdsman thou wert called,
But now thou seemest like a goatherd man
That gazes on the she-goats and their loves
With tear-worn eyes that he is not a goat.
(Lead, Muses, lead our rural melody.)
So thou, because thou seest the girls at play,
Hast tear-worn eyes because thou play'st not with
them."
But answer made he none to all of this,
Hoarding his bitter love until the end.
Lead, Muses, lead our rural melody.
Came Cypris with soft smiles,—a subtle smile,
For wrath was in her heart,—and said, " Wert he,
Daphnis, wert he that boasted against love,
He was love's master ? art not now thyself
Mastered and thrown by most untoward love?"
Lead, Muses, lead our rural melody.
And then he answered : " Cypris the oppressor,
Cypris the vengeful, Cypris enemy
Of mortal men, now sayest thou indeed
That all my sun is set, and even below
Daphnis shall be a pitiful wreck of love."
Lead, Muses, lead our rural melody.

G

" Go then to Ida, where thy herdsman claspt
His Cypris,—to Anchises ; there are oaks
Wide-spreading : here is only galingale,
Here bees make gentle murmur round their hives."

Lead, Muses, lead our rural melody.
" Or to Adonis, where he feeds his flocks,
And strikes the hare, and chases forest-game."

Lead, Muses, lead our rural melody.
" Then face once more Tydides' spear, and vaunt,
' I conquer shepherd Daphnis ; fight thou too.'"

Lead, Muses, lead our rural melody.
" Farewell, ye lynxes, and ye wolves, farewell!
Ye bears that lurk in mountain-glens, farewell!
No more will Daphnis to the forest come,
Nor in the oakwoods will he see you more,
Nor in the copses ;—and thou too, farewell,
Fountain of Arethusa! and ye streams
That to the tide of Thymbris hurry down!"

Lead, Muses, lead our rural melody.
" Lo ! I am Daphnis, who fed oxen here,
And here led bulls and heifers to the well."

Lead, Muses, lead our rural melody.
" O Pan, god Pan, whether thou restest now
Upon the mountain-ridges of Lycæus,
Or roamest round huge Mænalus, come hence
To this Sicilian isle, and leave the cliffs
Of Helicé, and that star-pointed tomb,
Beloved by gods, of old Lycaon's son."

Cease, Muses, cease our rural melody.
" Hither, my king, and this sweet-sounding pipe,
Moulded to fit these lips, and fashioned well
With pliant wax,—O, take it; for I go,
For love's sake unto Hades am I drawn."

    Cease, Muses, cease our rural melody.
" Ye thorns, ye brambles, now be blossomed o'er
With violets, and thou, fair daffodil,
Bloom on a juniper, and pines drop pears,
And all belie its nature; for he dies,
For Daphnis dies; then let stags capture hounds,
And mountain owls try notes with nightingales!"

    Cease, Muses, cease our rural melody.
With this he closed. And Aphrodité strove
To lift him up; but all the threads of life
Were forfeit to the Fates.—And so he passed
The sullen stream whose waters overwhelm'd
The darling of the Muses and the Nymphs.

    Cease, Muses, cease our rural melody.
Now give the goat, and give the drinking-cup,
And I will milk and to the Muses pour
Libation due. Hail, Muses, ever hail!
To-morrow will I sing a sweeter song.

HERDSMAN.

Filled be thy fair mouth, Thyrsis, evermore
With honey and the honeycomb. Thy food
Be luscious figs fresh-plucked in Ægilus!

Thou sing'st more sweetly than cicadas sing.
Here is the goblet.—Friend, how sweet it smells !
Surely thou well might'st deem it had been dipped
And washed amid the fountains of the Hours.
Hither, Cissætha.—Milk her, friend ;—and ye,
Skip not, young kidlings, lest your lord appear.

IDYL II.

The Enchantress.

WHERE are my laurels? bring them, Thestylis;
My philtres too;—enfold yon drinking-cup
In choicest crimson wool, that over him,
Dear cause of all my hurt, I may assert
The power of spells, because for twice six days
He has kept cruel absence, knowing not
Whether I live or die; nor at my door—
Hard-hearted—has he knocked; perhaps for him
Another home has fickle Eros found,
And Aphrodité. I will seek at morn
The athlete's haunt in Timagetus' school,
And I will look on him, and speak reproach
For all that he has done. But now with rites
Of magic I devote him. Shine, shine bright,
Selené; unto thee a whispered chaunt
I will upraise, and unto Hecaté

Of the nether world; before whose felt approach
Through dead men's tombs and rivers of black blood
Dogs cower and quake. Terrible Hecaté,
Be favourable! help me to the end,
And make my spells of no less efficacy
Than Circé's or Medea's, or the drugs
Of Perimedé with the flaxen hair.

Wheel, draw my lover to my arms again.
First in the fire the barley-meal is wasted.
Sprinkle it, Thestylis. Coward, whence has fled
Thy courage? am I even to thee, O wretch,
A laughing-stock?—I tell thee, sprinkle it,
And say the while, "I sprinkle Delphis' bones."

Wheel, draw my lover to my arms again.
Delphis has wrought me woe: so I for him
Let burn this laurel, which, enwrapped in fire,
Crackles amain, and blazing instantly,
Leaves not an ash behind; so may the flesh
Of Delphis vanish utterly in flame!

Wheel, draw my lover to my arms again.
As, under ghostly aid, this taper wastes,
May Myndian Delphis with consuming love
Be likewise wasted; as this brazen sphere,
By Aphrodité's favour, speeds along,
So he be sped a suppliant to my door!

Wheel, draw my lover to my arms again.
Now burn the bran. Thou, Artemis, canst move
Th' infernal adamant, and whatsoe'er

Is stubbornest. Hark! up and down the city
The dogs howl at us, Thestylis. The goddess
Sits in the crossways. Quick, the cymbals clash.

Wheel, draw my lover to my arms again.
The sea is silent now, the winds are still,
But not the grief within my heart is still,
For I am all on fire for him, by whom
I live in shame—no virgin, yet no wife.

Wheel, draw my lover to my arms again.
Thrice the libation falls, and thrice to thee,
Goddess, I pray. Whoe'er his now delight,
Or boy or maid, may lethé be his lot,
Forgotten, as they say in Naxos once
Theseus forgot his fair-haired Ariadné.

Wheel, draw my lover to my arms again.
There is a plant in Arcady that stirs
The steed to frenzy. O'er the mountain slopes
Colts and fleet mares rage maddened with its juice.
So may he leave the shining gymnast throng,
And seek a home here with like frenzied heart!

Wheel, draw my lover to my arms again.
Here is the fringe of Delphis' robe. He left it.
And I, behold, I tear it into shreds,
And hurl it in fierce fire. Love, ay me!
O grievous love, why, like a marish leech,
Suck'st thou the very life-blood from my veins?

Wheel, draw my lover to my arms again.
I pound a lizard, so a noxious draught

May reach thee in the morning.—Thestylis,
Take up these poisons, sprinkle them, and smear
To the very top his door-posts, unto which
Even now my soul is chained; but he, alas!
Makes no account of me!—spit banefully,
And say the while, "Thus smear I Delphis' bones!"

Wheel, draw my lover to my arms again.
Now all alone how shall I weep my love?
Whence date my story? who worked me this woe?
The daughter of Eubulus came one day,
Anaxo, to the grove of Artemis,
Carrying a votive basket. All around
Went in procession wild beasts many a one,
And in their midst a single lioness.

Goddess Selené, tell my love's sad tale.
A Thracian, daughter of Theucharilas,—
Erewhile my nurse, but now among the blest,—
Who dwelt hard by, prayed and petitioned me
To go and view the sight. And I, woe's me!
I followed, drawing on my linen vest,
And round my shoulders Clearista's cloak.

Goddess Selené, tell my love's sad tale.
Halfway along the road, near Lycon's house,
Delphis and Eudamippus walked together.
I saw them; and the colour of their beards
Was fairer than the flower of helichryse;
And fresh from strife of wholesome exercise,
Their breasts shone brighter than thy own bright beams.

Goddess Selené, tell my love's sad tale.
And when I looked upon him, I was struck
With frenzy; through and through my heart was
    pierced,
And all my colour faded ; from my eyes
Pomp and procession vanished, and somehow,
I know not how, I reached my home ; for fire
Consumed me utterly, and on my couch
For ten days and ten nights I lay as dead.

Goddess Selené, tell my love's sad tale.
My skin became like saffron-staining wood,
The hair fell from my head, and I remained
But bones and skin. Say, went not I to all,
Say, passed I by one single sorceress ?
But there was none to help. And time sped on.

Goddess Selené, tell my love's sad tale.
Then to my slave I opened all the truth :
" Go, Thestylis, find me some remedy
For this sad evil. All my very being
Is wrapped up in this Myndian. Go, then,
And watch the wrestling-school of Timagetus,
That he frequents, and there he loves to lounge."

Goddess Selené, tell my love's sad tale.
" And when thou seest him all alone, just touch him,
And whisper softly, ' 'Tis Simætha calls thee,'
And bring him hither privily."—This I said.
So went she, and anon brought to my door

Fair radiant Delphis. But when I beheld
His light foot just upon the threshold-gate,

(Goddess Selené, tell my love's sad tale.)
I turned all chill, more chill than frozen snow,
And down my face, like showers of rain, there ran
A stream of sweat, nor could I say a word,
Not even as much as infants in their sleep,
Who stammer to their mother; but I stood
Motionless, like a doll, and colourless.

Goddess Selené, tell my love's sad tale.
He with no love looked at me, on the bed
Sat down, and fixed his eyes on earth, and spoke.
" Truly, Simætha, thou wert just before me,
In summoning me hither, much as I
Pursued the fair Philinus once, and caught,
And in like way anticipated him."

Goddess Selené, tell my love's sad tale.
" For surely I had come, sweet love be witness,
With two or three companions I had come
This very night, with apples in my lap
Of Dionysus, and upon my head
White poplar, leaf beloved of Heracles,
With purple fillets all engarlanded."

Goddess Selené, tell my love's sad tale.
" And hadst thou welcomed me, then all were well;
For I am agile, and from all my feres
Bear off the palm of beauty; I had slept,

If only I could kiss thy darling lips.
But hadst thou pushed me off, and barred the door,
Then from all sides had torches lit the attack,
And with sharp axes I had forced an entrance."

  Goddess Selené, tell my love's sad tale.
" Now say I that the debt of thanks is due
To Cypris first, and after Cypris next
To thee, fair mistress, who hast called me here,
And snatched me from the fire, that has well-nigh
Devoured me.   For the fires that Love excites
Beat all Hephæstus' flames in Lipara,

  (Goddess Selené, tell my love's sad tale.)
And drive the frenzied virgin from her couch,
And from the yet warm pillows of her lord
Make flee the bride."—And this was all he said;
And I believed him easily, and took
His hand, and sank upon the bed of down,
And soon flesh warmed to flesh, and in our cheeks
There came a glow that had not come before,
And each to each we breathed soft whisperings ;
And, not to talk too much, Selené blest,
The sum was summed, and both had our desire.
And up to yesterday nor he found fault
With me, nor I with him ; but came to-day,—
What time those steeds clomb heaven, and lifted up
Aurora rosy-fingered from the sea,—
The mother of my flute-girl, Philista,
And of Melixo, telling me much news,

And with it, how that Delphis was in love.
But whether boy or maid had stolen his heart,
She did not know for certain; only this,
That evermore he drank of love's pure wine,
And now had fled, and never to return.
And also that his house was all enwreathed
With garlands; this she told me when she came.
And it is true, I know; for he had been
Often and often, bringing me betimes
A Dorian oil-flask. Now twelve days have gone
Since last I saw him.—Has he then some charm,
Some fresh delight? and am I then forgot?
Therefore I will compel him with my spells,
And save he spare to grieve me, he shall knock,
By the Erinnyes, he shall knock at the gate of Hell.
Such deadly poisons do I keep for him,
Locked up in a casket, mingled by the rules
Of an Assyrian sorceress.—But thou,
Goddess, all hail, and bid thy coursers speed
Towards Ocean. I will go and work the work
To which I set myself.—Selené, hail!
Bright white Selené,—and ye other stars
That circle round the car of silent Night.

IDYL III.

Amaryllis.

I SING to Amaryllis, while my goats
Feed on the mountain-sides, and Tityrus
Directs their course. Belovèd Tityrus,
Pasture them well, and lead them to the fount;
But watch that pale white goat from Libya,
Lord of the harem, lest he butt at thee.

    Ay me! fair Amaryllis, wilt thou not
Peep from thy cave again, and call once more
Thy too-fond lover?—sure thou hat'st not him?

    Surely I seem not, when I stand before thee,
Flat-nosed and satyr-chinned?—I shall go hang.

    Here are ten apples: where thou bad'st me pluck
I plucked them, and to-morrow will bring more.

    Look on my bitter woe; would Heaven I were
A murmurous bee to enter in thy cave,
Flitting among the ivy and the fern
That shades thee round!

　　　　　　　　　Now know I Love indeed,—
A stern hard god.　A lioness gave him milk,
And in oak-thickets was he nurturèd.
He wastes me now and burns me to the bone.

　　O sweet, sweet eyes ! O stony, stony heart !
O maiden of dark eyebrows, stretch thy arms,
And clasp me while. I kiss thee !—empty kiss !
But even in empty kisses there is joy.

　　Ah ! thou wilt make me tear up into shreds
This ivy-wreath that I have kept for thee,—
For thee, sweet Amaryllis, and have twined
Rich ivy fruit and parsley odorous.

　　Alas my woes ! alas my ruined life !
Wilt thou not listen ?—then will I strip off
My shepherd-garb, and leap into the waves
Where fisher Olpis keeps look-out for tunnies ;
And if I die not, yet to have tried to die
Will give thee pleasure.

　　　　　　　　　Long ago I knew,
What time I tried the question of thy love,
And poppy-leaves were folded round my arm,—
But no sound came, and on my tender skin
They withered all away.

　　　　　　　　　Also there came
A gleaner-girl, Agroeo, from the throng
Of harvesters, and augured by the sieve,
And spoke the truth, that all my heart and soul
Would hang on thee, and thou wouldst slight my love.

　　Look how I keep a milk-white goat for thee,

Mother of twins : a dark-skinned servant-maid,
Daughter of Mermnon, begs it ; she shall have it,
Since thou mak'st game of me.

                My right eye throbs :
Say, shall I see her ?—I will lay me down
By yonder pine, and sing, and she perchance
Will see me, since she is not adamant.

    Seeking a virgin bride, Hippomenes
Took apples in his hand, and ran the course ;
But Atalanta,—how she gazed and burned,
How leapt she headlong into love's abyss!

    The seer Melampus drove from Othrys' mount
His herds to Pylos, while the mother fair
Of wise Alphesibœa lay embraced
In Bias' arms.

             Adonis in like way,
Tending his flocks along the mountain-sides,
Frenzied he not fair Cytherea, so
That even when dead she clasped him to her breast?

    Happy Endymion, an eternal sleep
Thou sleepest! Happy too Iasion,
Who shared such joys as ribalds may not know.

    My head throbs ; but it matters not to her.
I will not sing again. Here will I fall,
Here will I lie, and wolves devour me :
That too shall be like honey in her throat.

IDYL IV.

———— –

BATTUS.

WHOSE are these cattle? tell me, Corydon;
Philondas's?

CORYDON.

No; Ægon's, who himself
Bade me come feed them.

BATTUS.

Friend, at eventide
Hast anywhere to milk them on the quiet?

CORYDON.

No; for the old man puts the calves to suck,
And keeps good watch on me.

BATTUS.

And he, our shepherd,
Whither away has he fled?

CORYDON.

Hast not heard ?
Milo has taken him to Alpheus' banks.

BATTUS.

When then did *his* eyes chance to light on oil ?

CORYDON.

They say his thews were match for Heracles.

BATTUS.

My mother said *I* could beat Polydeuces.

CORYDON.

He took his hoe, and twenty of these sheep.

BATTUS.

Milo forsooth will set the wolves on raging.

CORYDON.

Hear how those heifers low and long for him!

BATTUS.

Poor things, a wretched shepherd have they found !

CORYDON.

Poor things indeed, they care not even to eat !

BATTUS.

Look at that cow ; there's nothing left of her
But bones ! pray does she chance to dine off dew,
Like a cicada ?

CORYDON.

No, by mother Earth !
Sometimes I pasture her near Æsarus,

H

And give her a good wisp of tender hay ;
At other times she gambols in the shade
Around Latymnus.

BATTUS.

Then there's the roan bull,
How lean he looks !—please Heaven the Lampriads
Have such a victim, when they sacrifice
To Heré ! for they *are* a noxious lot.

CORYDON.

He too is driven to the estuary,
And to the parts of Physcus and Neæthus
Where grows the best of herbage, ægipyre,
Flea-bane, and odorous baulm.

BATTUS.

Ah, well-a-day !
Poor Ægon, that thy precious herds must go
To Hades, while thou aim'st at victory—
A losing victory ; and this poor pipe,
Made long ago by thee, is specked with mould.

CORYDON.

Not it, by the Nymphs ! for, when he left for Pisa,
He gave it me ; and I am musical,
And I can strike up famously the songs
Of Glauca and of Pyrrhus.   Croton town
I celebrate ; Zacynthus too is fair;
So is Lacinium's promontory,
That faces morning, where our athlete Ægon
For a single meal ate eighty barley-cakes.

And from the mountain there he dragged a bull,
Hoof-held, for Amaryllis ; from afar
Shouted the women, and the herdsman laughed.

BATTUS.

Yes, charming Amaryllis, thou alone,
Though dead, art not forgotten.   Dear to me
As are my goats is thy loved memory.
Alas ! the hard hard fate that is my lot.

CORYDON.

Cheer up, friend Battus, and to-morrow's sun
Will bring thee, by good chance, some better luck.
While there is life, there's hope ; the dead alone
Are hopeless.   Zeus sends sunshine when he wills,
And when he wills he rains.

BATTUS.

                         Right.   I'll cheer up.
Send off those calves down there.   Curse them ! they
          gnaw
The olive-branches.   Whish ! be off, white-skin !

CORYDON.

Off there, Cymætha, to the mound !   What now !
Hearest thou not ? then will I come, by Pan,
And make thee suffer, if thou get not hence.
Look, here she comes again.   O, if I had
A good stout cudgel, trust me I would whack thee !

BATTUS.

Quick, Corydon ! in the name of Zeus ; a thorn
Has just pierced near my ancle.   Gods, how dense

These brambles are !   The heifer go to hell !
Through looking after her I got this hurt.
Seest thou the thorn ?

CORYDON.

Yes, yes ; I hold it now
Between my nails.   Look at it, here it is.

BATTUS.

A little harm ; but what a man it maims !

CORYDON.

Friend Battus, when thou walkest mountain-wards,
Don't go barefooted ; for upon the hill
Briers and prickly shrubs abound.

BATTUS.

Tell me,
O Corydon, does the old man still adore
That girl with the dark eyebrows, his old flame ?

CORYDON.

As much as ever, knave.   The other day
I chanced to pass the cave, and there they were ;
I caught him in the act.

BATTUS.

Bravo, old man !
A lecherous dog indeed ; in blood forsooth
Akin to Satyrs or the rough-legged Fauns.

IDYL VII.

The Walk in Spring.

TIME was that I strolled forth with Eucritus
To Haleus, from the town, and with us came
A third, Amyntas, when Antigenes
And Phrasidamus, sons of Lycopeus,
Kept first-fruit feast to Ceres; noble they,
If noble sires e'er yet got noble sons,
From Clytia sprung and Chalcon, who erewhile
Strove with bent knee against the rugged rock,
And bade the fountain of Burinna rise.
There elms and poplars make a shady bower,
And waving green leaves are its vaulted roof.

And not yet half accomplished was the way,
Nor yet in sight the tomb of Brasilas,
When, by the Muses' grace, we chanced to meet
A right good traveller, Lycidas by name,
A Cretan, and a goatherd; none could fail
To tell his calling, for from top to toe

He looked a goatherd; on his back he wore
A shaggy bristly he-goat's tawny skin,
Strong of fresh rennet, and an ancient cloak
Buckled across his chest; his right hand grasped
A gnarled wild-olive crook, and looking up
With quiet humour twinkling in his eye
He spoke, while laughter played upon his lip.
    "Simichidas, where drag thy noontide steps?
For now the lizard sleeps upon the wall,
The crested lark flits not from brow to brow.
Dost hurry to some board, a bidden guest?
Or to the trampling of some neighbour's grapes?
For sure thy booted feet so spurn the earth,
The very stones ring echo to thy tramp."
    And I made answer: "Thou, friend Lycidas,
Canst pipe, as all men say, like none beside,
Shepherd or reaper; this I hear with joy.
Yet, if I know aright, I may aspire
To be thy equal.   See now; we are bound
For the Thalysia; for friends of ours
To fair-robed Ceres offer sacrifice,
The first-fruits of their store, because for them
The goddess has filled floors and granaries
With bounteous yield of harvest.   Come, my friend,
The road, the day's our own; let song be ours.
One can support the other, and my tongue
Is fervid with the Muse; the common voice
Calls me a prince of bards; but I, in sooth,
I trust not that same voice too readily,

By mother Earth, not I ; for I know well
I could not beat Sicelidas in song,
The Samian, nor Philetas ; I should be
A frog against cicadas." Of design
I spoke : he with a pleasant smile rejoined :
  " This crook shall be thy guerdon, seeing Zeus
Hath fashioned thee in all things truth itself.
Odious to me the builder who desires
To raise a house high as Oromedon.
And so the Muses' warblers toil in vain
Who crow defiance to the Chian bard.
  " But come, Simichidas, haste to awake
The rural Muse ; I pray thee, give good heed,
So haply thou mayst like this melody
I wrought of late upon the mountain-side.
  ' Fair be the voyage for Ageanax, I pray,
To Mitylené, though the rainy south
Press on the billows, when the Goats are low,
And old Orion rests his foot i' the sea,
If fate would snatch from Aphrodité's fires
The wasted Lycidas ; fierce love for him
Consumes me ; halcyons shall lay the waves,
Shall still the sea, the south-wind, and the east
That stirs the furthest sea-wrack—halcyons
Beyond all birds by grey-green Nereïds
The best beloved, and peoples of the sea.
May all be fair and well for Ageanax,
And waft him sweetly to the wished-for port.
And I that day will wear upon my head

Wreath of anethum, or a garland-crown
Of roses or white violets, and quaff
From a deep flagon wine of Ptelea,
And by the fireside stretch myself to rest.
And one shall roast me beans amid the flame,
And one shall pile my bed a cubit high
With twining parsley and with asphodel
And flea-bane; I the while will drink at ease,
And toast Ageanax till to the cup
My lips cling fast and drain the very dregs.
And I will have two shepherds flute for me;
The one from Attica, Ætolian one;
And Tityrus shall stand beside, and sing
How Daphnis burned for Xenia long ago,
And how he roamed the mountain, and the oaks
Sighed dirges for him by the river-banks
Of Himera, what time he died away,
As dies a snow-flake upon Hæmus' top,
Athos, or Rhodope, or on the steeps
Of extreme Caucasus. And he shall sing
How a wide cage received a shepherd once,
Yet living, through the vile scorn of his lord,
And how into the odorous cedarn wood
Came, with soft blossoms out of flowery fields,
The honey-hiving bees, and nourished him,
Because the Muse poured nectar from his tongue.
Happy Comatas! happy was thy lot,
Prisoned within a cage, to wile away
The summer months, and feed on honeycomb!

O, wert thou numbered with the living now!
How would I tend fair she-goats on the hills
For thee! how would I listen for thy voice!
And thou, divine Comatas, wouldst repose
In shade of oaks or pines, and sweetly sing.'"
    With this he ceased, and I in turn replied :
" Full many a melody, friend Lycidas,
The Nymphs have taught me as I watched my herds
Among the mountain-valleys ; songs so rare
Their fame has borne them to the throne of Zeus.
But this is far the first, which I will sing
To do thee honour, and surpasses all ;
So listen, for thou art the Muses' friend.
    ' Ill-luck the Loves sneeze for Simichidas,
Who longs for blooming Myrto, woe is him!
As she-goats for the spring.   His dearest friend,
Aratus, his most trusted, in his heart
Yearns for the boy.   The good Aristis knows,
That best of men, whom singing to his lyre
Not Phœbus' self would from his tripods spurn,
What fierce love burns Aratus to the core.
But, king of the fair realm of Homolé,
I pray thee, Pan, let his arms clasp his love,
Albeit unsought for, whosoe'er he is,
Philinus or another ; for which boon,
Kind Pan, no vengeful boys of Arcady
Shall scourge thy back and shoulders with reed-rods,
When flesh is scarce on the altar.   This refused,
May sharp nails tear and scratch thee head to foot,

And nettles be thy bed ; and Thracian hills
Thy home in the mid-winter, near the stream
Of Hebrus, with thy face towards the Bear ;
And in the summer mayst thou feed thy flocks
Far off in Æthiopia, underneath
The Blemyan rocks, where none can see the Nile.
But ye, bright apple-rosy Loves, that haunt
Dioné's lofty shrine, O come away,
Leave the sweet fountains Byblis, Hyetis,
And pierce adored Philinus with your shafts,
O pierce him, for he pities not my friend,
The cruel scorner ; yet is he full ripe,
And waxing softer than a mellow pear.
' Ah, for Philinus,' all the women say,
'The blossom of thy beauty fades away !'
No more, Aratus, let us watch his door,
Pace no more weary journeys ; but at dawn
Crow chanticleer, and send some other wight
To dreary chills, and only one beside,
But Molon only suffer in this strife.
But peaceful rest for us, and some old witch
To spit at spells, and keep us clear of harm.' "
　　　I ended ; with a sweet smile, as before,
He gave the crook, the guerdon of the Muse.
Then, bending to the left, he took the road
To Pyxæ ; we to Phrasidamus' house,
The fair Amyntas, I, and Eucritus,
Wended our way.　There on a couch profuse
Of odorous mastich, and the fresh-cut shoots

Of vines, we lay in joy ; and overhead
Tall elms and poplars rustled in the breeze,
And bubbling upward from the Muses' grot
Murmured a sacred fountain at our side.
And chattering high amid the shady boughs
The sun-burnt cicales toiled their ceaseless song.
Far in the thickness of the briery bush
Harsh croaked the frog ; carolled the crested larks,
Carolled the linnets, and the wood-dove moaned,
And yellow bees around the fountains hummed.
All had a scent of bounteous summer, all
Savoured of rich ripe fruit-time. At our feet
Pears in profusion rolled, and by our side
Fell store of apples ; heavy-laden boughs
Bent down to earth with burden of their plums,
And from the cask the four-year seal was loosed.
Castalian nymphs, queens of Parnassus' height,
Did ever yet in Pholus' stony cave
Old Chiron place such cup for Heracles ?
Was e'er the shepherd of Anapus' banks,
The stalwart Polyphemus, who uptore
Mountains and hurled them against flying ships,
Moved by such nectar to lead out the dance,
And foot it through his sheepfolds, as that day
Ye caused to flow for us beside the shrine
Of Ceres, harvest-queen ? upon whose stacks
Oft may I fix again my winnow-fan ;
Oft may she smile, the while her fair hands hold
Sheaves with red poppies mingled in their midst.

IDYL XI.

Cyclops.

Nicias, I know no remedy for love,
No balsam, and no salve, except the Muse.
A soft sweet solace to the favoured ones,
But very hard to find.   This, as I think,
Physician as thou art, and dear beside
Unto the heavenly Nine, thou knowest well.

    Thus our Sicilian Cyclops wiled the hours,
Old Polypheme, when in the bloom of youth,
The down yet soft upon his lips and cheeks,
He burned for Galatea.   Roses then,
Apples, nor shining ringlets, showed his love,
But direful frenzies.   Everything beside
Counted as nothing.   Many a time his sheep
Back from the yellow meadows to their fold
Wandered at will ; he, chanting of his fair,
Sat by the weedy strand from dawn of day
Love-wasted, for a wound was in his heart,
And Cypris' shafts had pierced him through and through.

Then found he the one cure ; high on a rock
He sat, and gazing seaward sang this song :
  " Fair Galatea, why dost spurn my love ?
O whiter than pressed milk ! O softer far
Than any lamb, more skittish than a calf,
And harsher than a grape yet unmatured !
So ever comest thou what time sweet sleep
Doth hold me fast,—so straightway art thou gone
When sweet sleep sets me free, as flies a lamb
From sudden vision of a grisly wolf.
I loved thee, dear, I loved thee from the day
Thou camest with my mother long ago
To pluck the hyacinths on the mountain-sides.
I led the way, I saw thee ; from that hour
To this my love has ceased not : but, alas !
It matters not, it matters not to thee.
I know, sweet maid, the reason of thy flight ;
Because from ear to ear across my front
Stretches a shaggy eyebrow all in one,
And but a single eye flames underneath,
And my flat nose lies level with my lips.
Yet, for all that, a thousand flocks are mine,
Rich store of milk they yield me when I thirst ;
Nor in the summer do I lack for cheese,
In autumn, nor mid-winter ; evermore
My crates are overfull ; and I can pipe
As pipes no other Cyclops, and of thee
Oft at the dead of night, sweet rosy love,
I sing, and link thy name with mine in song.

For thee have I reared up eleven fawns,
And all are necklaced, and four little bears.
Come then to me; of all that I enjoy
Take equal share, and let the grey-green sea
Go tumble as it will upon the shore.
Thy sleep will be much sweeter by my side
In yonder grot; for laurel-groves are there,
Tall cypresses are there, and ivy dark,
And vines rich loaded with the luscious grape;
There is cool water, that from her pure snows
Thick-wooded Ætna sends me, drink divine.
Who would prefer to these the ocean-wave?
Yet, if I seem fierce-looking and uncouth,
There are oak-logs, and sparks of living fire
Among the ashes; burn me if thou wilt,
My heart is burnt even now, and my one eye,
My blessed eye may burn; I will not flinch.
Ay me! had I been only born with fins
To plunge into the waves, and kiss thy hand,
If hindered from thy lips; I would have brought
White lilies, and the red broad-petalled bloom
Of tender poppies; nay, I could not bring
The two at once, for summer flowers are these,
And those of winter: now if some chance ship
Would bear a voyager hither, I would learn
To swim, and I would find what rare delight
Is yours to dwell among the ocean-depths.
Come, Galatea, and, once come, forget,
As I forget here sitting, to return.

O stay with me, and tend the flocks, and milk,
Stir in sharp rennet, and compress the cheese.
It is my mother who is doing me wrong,
My mother only ; she is all to blame.
From day to day she sees me pine away,
But speaks not a kind word in my behalf
To make thee love me. I will let her know
How my head throbs, how weary are my feet,
That she may suffer ; for I suffer sore.
O Cyclops, Cyclops, whither has flown thy wit ?
Go home and weave thy baskets, cut fresh leaves
And give them to thy lambs ; 'twill show perchance
Much sounder sense ; enjoy thy present good :
Why trouble to pursue a fleeting love ?
Another Galatea thou mayst find,
Perhaps a fairer ; many a young maid
Bids me to nightly frolics, and they laugh,
All titter, if I do but listen to them.
Clearly they think me here of some account."

  Thus Polypheme beguiled his love with song :
A better medicine were not bought with gold.

IDYL XII.

The Beloved.

———

AFTER two morns and nights, loved one, thou comest;
But those that long grow agèd in a day.
Better than winter as the fresh spring-time,
Sweeter than sloes as apples,—as a sheep
Is fleecier than her lamb, and as a maid
Is better far than a thrice-married wife,
And fleeter than a heifer as a fawn;
As of all birds the clear-voiced nightingale
Sings sweetest far; so am I gladdened most
When thou art here; and so I run to thee
As runs some traveller from the scorching ray
Under a shady oak. May equal Loves
Breathe kindly on us both, and may we live
A theme of song to late posterity:
" Such were two men, the lights of by-gone days,
A lover one (as Spartan tongues would have it),

And one beloved (Thessalians would say);
An equal love bound each. Ah, then, be sure
Were golden men, when the loved loved again."

Would this were so, O father Chronides !
Then should we be exempt from age and death.
Or else, two hundred generations gone,
Come one to Acheron impassable
And herald this : " Thy love, and his, thy own,
Thy darling's, lives upon the lips of all,
And most of all the youthful."

As for this,
The heavenly ones, the rulers of events,
Will work their will ; but I, who hail thee fair,
Blow no lie-blisters on my nostril-arch.
And if thou do me wrong, thou mak'st the wrong
No wrong, but double bounty ; and I go
With overflowing measure to my home.

O sons of Nisus, men of Megara,
Surpassing oarsmen, may your homes be blest,
Because ye honoured with exceeding mark
An Attic guest, the lover Diocles !
In the first days of spring for evermore
A throng of boys crowd round about his tomb
To win the prize of kissing ; he who can
Glue lip to lip most sweetly shall return
Smothered in flower-crowns to his mother's arms.
Happy is he who sits among those boys
As judge of kisses ;—surely he invokes

I

The frequent aid of blue-eyed Ganymede,
That he may have a mouth like Lydian stone,
With which the money-changers question gold,
And prove it, whether it be pure or false.

IDYL XIII.

Hylas.

Not, as we deemed, for us, friend Nicias,
Not for us only, that are born to die,
And look not to behold to-morrow's sun,
Was Love brought forth, what god soe'er he be
That claims his parentage, nor we the first
Love-lighted to the fairness of fair things,
But he, Amphitryon's iron-hearted son,
That bode the lion's onset, he too loved
Hylas the graceful with the curling hair,
And taught him all, as fathers teach their sons,
Whereby himself had grown to name and fame;
Nor left his side at midday, or when Morn
Drives her white coursers to the dome of Zeus,
Or when the callow nestlings look for rest,
And cheep and twitter when the parent wings
Flutter and spread above the sun-burnt perch:

That so when furnished to his heart's desire,
He might weigh heavy in the scales of right,
And issue in a very perfect man.

    Now when the son of Æson thought to sail
After the golden fleece, and many a chief,
The crown of all the cities, followed him
According to his need, there also came
To rich Iolchos the enduring son
Of Midean Alcmena, hero-queen ;
With whom descended Hylas to the shore
Where lay the bulwarked Argo, that alone
Grazed not the clashing cliffs Cyanean,
But shot betwixt, and, as with eagle's wing,
Swooped down on Phasis and the gulf's expanse,
And afterward the evil rocks stood still.
But when in heaven the Pleiades are high,
And spring is on the wane, and every field
Blossoms with pasture for the tender lambs,
Then did the godlike flower of hero kings
Bethink them of their sailing, and took seat
Within the hollow Argo, and three days
The south-wind wafted them to Hellespont,
Till in Propontis, where the toiling kine
Broaden the furrows of Cianian fields,
The anchor dropped ; they, landing on the shore,
Spread two and two the feast at eventide.
One couch was piled for many, for at hand
Lay a great pasture to supply their bed.
Tall spiry rushes and lush galingale

They carried thence, and Hylas golden-haired
Went to draw water for the evening meal,—
For Hercules, and Telamon the stern,
That ever sat beside the selfsame board,—
Bearing a brazen pitcher. And anon
He spied a fountain in a bosky dell ;
And many a marish nursling grew thereby,
Dark celandine, and pale light maiden-hair,
Twists of couch-grass, and parsley evergreen :
And in the midst the Nymphs their revels held,
Malis, Eunica, ever-wakeful nymphs,
Goddesses feared by all the country folk,
And young Nychia with a smile like spring.
Then stooped the boy his pitcher to the fount,
Intent to plunge it in :—they, one and all,
Hung on his hands ; soft hearts of one and all
Were wrung with passion for the Argive boy.
Sheer down he fell into the darksome wave,
Like as when falls from heaven a fiery star
Sheer down to ocean ; and some mariner
Calls to his fellows, " Gently there, my mates ;
Up with the sails ; there comes a fav'ring breeze."
Then holding in their lap the weeping boy,
The Nymphs consoled him with endearing words :
But in disquiet rose Amphitryon's son,
Holding in Scythian form his bended bow,
Holding the club that never left his grasp ;
Thrice to the fullest depth of his deep voice
He shouted " Hylas !" thrice the boy replied :

Thrice from the water came an empty sound,
And far away he seemed, though close at hand.
As when a lion with great fell of mane,
Rav'ning and raging in a mountain glen,
Catches far off the whimper of a fawn,
Springs from his lair, and to the timely feast
Rushes amain : so, yearning for his love,
Through many a briary and untravelled way
Raged Hercules, and compassed many a mile.
Unhappy lovers! how he toiled and roamed
Up many a mountain and through many a wood!
Jason and Jason's cause were all forgot.
There lay the ship ; the masts rose high in air ;
In the night-hours the young men trimmed the sails,
Till Hercules should come. But he the while
Where his feet led him wandered far away
In frenzy ; for a fierce god tore his heart.
Thus with th' immortals Hylas passing fair
Was numbered. And because he left the ship,
Faithless to Argo of the thirty oars,
The heroes scoffed at Hercules : but he
Strode on to Colchos and the sullen sea.

IDYL XV.

The Adoniazusæ.

GORGO.

At home, Praxinoë?

PRAXINOE.

Gorgo dear, at home;
After such absence!—well, the wonder is
You're here even now.—Eunoë, look out a chair,
And place a pillow.

GORGO.

Thanks, thanks;—not for me.

PRAXINOE.

Sit down, I beg.

GORGO.

Well! what I *have* gone through,
Without defeat!—you've got me just alive,
Praxinoë; such crowds, such chariot-hosts!
Nothing all round but booted soldiery,

And tunicked troops of horsemen ;—then the road—
Interminable ! you live in such a place,
So far from me !

PRAXINOE.

This is that idiot's work,
Who came to the world's end, and took this den,
A hovel, not a house,—to keep us two
From being neighbours ; always just the same,
Thwarting and grudging !

GORGO.

Fie, dear ; speak not so
About your husband Dinon, while the child
Is here.   Look how he's staring.—Never mind,
Zopyrion sweet, she does not mean papa.—
Well, by Persephoné, the young one sees
Your meaning.—Nice papa, dear, good papa !

PRAXINOE.

Our good papa set out the other day
(For any day may mean the other day)
To buy some rouge and soda at the shop,
And brought back—salt ! So clever for a man
Of thirteen cubits' stature !

GORGO.

Much the same
My spendthrift Diocleidas ; yesterday
He buys five fleeces, rubbish every one,
Washed and re-washed to shreds,—dog-fleeces they,
Old mangy scrapings ;—and he pays for them

Seven drachmæ!—Let us go ; put on your dress,
Fasten your shawl ; we'll seek the palace courts
Of Ptolemy the splendid, and behold
The Adonis ; for the queen, I hear, has planned
A lovely fête.

PRAXINOE.

Yes, in a lordly house
All things are lordly. All that you have seen
Tell me, who have seen nothing. Time enough
To go there.*

GORGO.

Yes ; it's always holiday
To those with nought to do.

PRAXINOE.

Come, Eunoë,
Pick up the yarn, and place it, lazy one,
Back by our side ; cats like a bed so soft.
Be quick, bring water,—water first of all.—
She's bringing soap !—Well, leave it ; pour away,
But not so fast, impatience ;—O you wretch,
You've wet my dress all over :—stop, leave off.
I'm washed somehow, as heaven has willed, it seems !—
Where is my key, the key of the big chest ?
Bring it.

* It is almost impossible to apportion the dialogue to the
speakers with any certainty. Almost every edition suggests
a different division.

GORGO.

Praxinoë dear, that folded shawl
And brooch is really charming. Tell me now
For how much *this* descended from the loom ?

PRAXINOE.

Don't think about it, Gorgo ;—more than one
Perhaps, yes, more than two pounds of fine gold ;
But then my heart and soul was in the work.

GORGO.

And surely the result is all you wish ?

PRAXINOE.

Yes, you say right, dear.—Eunoë, my mantle ;—
Put on my sun-shade neatly.—No, child, no,
I sha'nt take you.   Bah! bah! the horse will bite
  him!
Cry just as much as you like ; we can't afford
To have you lamed.—We *must* go.—Phrygia,
Take up the little one, and play with him;
Call the dog in, and fasten up the door.—
Heavens, what a crowd !—how ever shall we thread
This mass, unnumbered and illimitable
As ants ?—Full many a brave work hast thou done,
King Ptolemy, since thy good sire has been
Among the immortals.   Never a scoundrel now
Assaults the traveller, creeping stealthily
As do Egyptians, playing the base sports
Of by-gone men, moulded of trickeries,
Like each to each, the scum of humankind.—

Sweet Gorgo, what will happen? only see
The king's war-horses!—Good man, don't, I pray,
Tread on me!—There's the roan straight up in the air;
How wild he looks!—You shameless Eunoë,
Going to run away?—I'm sure he'll kill
His driver. Heaven be praised I left the child
Indoors!

GORGO.

Praxinoë, never mind; we're far
Behind them now. They're off to their own place.

PRAXINOE.

I'm rallying now. My horror from a child
Has been a horse, and a cold clammy snake.
We'll hurry on. What crowds are in our way!

GORGO.

From the palace, mother?

OLD WOMAN.

Even so, my child.

GORGO.

Is it easy to get in?

OLD WOMAN.

My pretty dears,
The Greeks got into Troy by trying hard:
By trying people may do everything.

GORGO.

The old lady spoke her oracle, and went.

PRAXINOE.

Women know everything, including even

How Zeus wed Herè.

GORGO.

Look, Praxinoë,
What a throng about the gates !

PRAXINOE.

Most wonderful !—
Gorgo, give me your hand.—Eunoë, give yours
To Eutychis ; take hold of her ; don't stray.
March all together ; I say, Eunoë,
Hold tight.—Ah me ! Gorgo, my summer vest
Is torn in two.—Man, if you hope for heaven,
In the name of Zeus, take care of my poor dress.

STRANGER.

Truly I haven't got it ;—all the same
I'll take good care.

PRAXINOE.

Look what a wedged-in mass ;
They push like hogs !

STRANGER.

Good lady, never fear ;
We're safe enough.

PRAXINOE.

This year, and evermore,
Kind man, may you continue safe and sound,
Who shielded me, like one compassionate
And well-disposed.—Here's Eunoë swept along,

Right over me.—Now, stupid, push away!—
That's capital!—all in;—as the man said
Who'd just locked out the bride.

GORGO.

Praxinoë,
Come here : look first at yonder tap'stry work;
How light, how graceful ! fit to clothe a god !

PRAXINOE.

August Athené, of what cunning maids
Is this the labour? and what artist-hands
Have wrought these life-like pictures ? How they're
            fixed
In actual presence ! how they intertwine
In actual play of limb ! They live, they breathe;
They are not woven.   A clever creature man !—
And he himself, in sight of every eye,
See how he lies upon his silver couch,
The tender down below his temples showing,
Adonis ever-loved, and loved as much
Beside the banks of Acheron !

SECOND STRANGER.

Give over,
Troublesome creatures, chattering without end,
Like wood-pigeons ; you wear all patience out,
Broadening your local twang on every word.

GORGO.

Well, mother Earth, whence did this worthy spring ?
What is it to you if we are garrulous?

Get your own slaves, and order them ;—think you
To order Syracusans ?—know besides
Our lineage is Corinthian, just as was
Bellerophon's ;—the language that we speak,
Of Peloponnesus ; and it is allowed
For Dorians to speak Doric, I believe.

PRAXINOE.

O Melitodes, let not any man
But one dictate to us : not that I care.
Don't think to throw your empty measures at me !

GORGO.

Silence, Praxinoë. The Argive maid,
The accomplished songstress, she who all surpassed,
The plaintive Sperchis, meditates a strain
In honour of Adonis ; well I know
She will give utterance to some melody
Of trancing note ; she's tuning up already.

SINGING-WOMAN.

Mistress, to whom Idalium is dear,
Golgi, and Eryx' steep,—O Aphrodité
The golden,—how the gentle-footed Hours
Have brought thee thy Adonis this twelfth month
From ever-flowing Acheron ! slow sweet Hours,
Slowest of heavenly ones, they come at last,
Much wished-for, bearing with them evermore
Some gift for mortal men. O Cypris, thou,
Dioné's child, didst take, as story goes,

A mortal, Berenicé, and didst feed
Her mortal body with ambrosial food,
And madest her immortal; and for this,
Her daughter, fair as Helen, Arsinoë,
Gives gifts to thee, goddess of many names
And many shrines, and decks with offerings fair
Thy own Adonis. By his side are placed
All fruits that ripen on the forest-boughs,
Soft plants in fence of silver filigree,
And golden caskets filled with Syrian nard,
And every pastry-work of cunning mould,
Where flowers of all hues mingle with white meal;
And all that flies and all that creeps is there,
Moulded with luscious honey in liquid oil.
And there pale bowers are builded, shaded round
With soft anethum; and young Loves above
Flit to and fro, like nightingales new-fledged,
That try their wings i' the woods from bough to bough.
O look! the ebony—O look! the gold;
The eagles of white ivory, that lift
The boy cupbearer to the throne of Zeus;
And see the purple carpets higher up,
" Softer than sleep" (Milesian tongues would say,
Or men of Samos). There a couch is spread
For fair Adonis; one for Cypris, one
For rosy-armed Adonis ;—'tis a spouse
Of eighteen years or nineteen; and his kiss
Carries no smart, for still the blush of youth
Mantles around his lips. Hail, Cypris, hail !

Now take thy fill of love!

And we will go
Together in the morning, while the dew
Still shines, and lay him down beside the waves
That foam along the strand, and loose our hair,
And drop our garments to our feet, and stand
With bosoms bared, and raise our plaintive chant:

"Beloved Adonis, thou dost come and go
From here to Acheron, like none beside
Of godlike men: not Agamemnon's self
Obtained that favour, nor the heroic bulk
Of Ajax stung with frenzy; no, nor he,
Far noblest of all Hecabe's twenty sons,
Not Hector; not Patroclus; nor who voyaged
Homeward from Troy, not Pyrrhus; not who lived
Long earlier, the Lapithæ, or stock
Of old Deucalion; nor Pelasgic sires,
The crown of Argos and Thessalian state.
Now, loved Adonis, look propitiously,
And bring us blessings in the coming year.
Benignly hast thou visited us now,
Benignly come again!"

GORGO.

Praxinoë dear,
Woman's the cleverer creature, after all.
Happy to know so much; but happier still
To sing so sweetly.—Now 'tis time for home;
Diocleidas hasn't dined; and he's a man

At all times passionate ; but when he's hungry
Go nowhere near him.

     Farewell, best-beloved
Adonis ! thou hast been with greeting friends.

IDYL XX.

Eunica.

———

EUNICA, whom I dearly long to love,
Laughs me to scorn, and thus with mocking tongue
Launches her speech : " Away from me ; begone !
Dost thou, a herdsman, think to kiss me, *me,*—
Poor fool, who never learned of rustic love,
But only how to press a high-born lip !
By heaven, thou shalt not kiss my pretty mouth,
Not even in dreams. Why, what a fright thou lookest !
What things thou sayest ! how boorish is thy play !
How silly-soft thy tongue ! what stuff it babbles !
Thy chin is smooth : thy hair is like a girl's :
Thy lips are nasty, and thy hands are black :
Thy smell is not too sweet ;—go—soil not me !"
This said, she spat three times into her breast,
And looked me over well from head to foot,
With lips well-shaped to sneer, and eye askance ;

And turned and twirled her body to and fro,
Coquette-like; laughing at me as she turned,
Showing her teeth, and strutting haughtily.
But as for me, my blood began to boil,
My skin flushed crimson with the pain, as a rose
Flushes with morning dew. And she passed on,
And left me; but within my heart I rage,
That *me* the graceful, me the blooming fair
This evil mistress does revile and spurn.

    Ye shepherds, tell me true : am I not fair ?
Or has some god worked any sudden change,
And made me some one else ? for erst I bloomed
With beauty, that just bursting into bloom,
Clothed all my chin, as ivy clothes a tree.
My hair, like wreathing parsley, streamed in waves
About my temples ; and my forehead shone
White, over night-black brows ; more deeply blue
My eyes and brighter than Athené's own ;
Softer my mouth than cream new-pressed to cheese ;
And sweet the words that trickle from my lips,
Sweeter than honey from the honeycomb ;
And sweet my music,—whether on the pipe
I play, or on the flute sweet sounds discourse,
Or on the reed, or on the double-flute.
And all the hill-side women call me fair,
All love me ; but this town-girl loves me not.
She, for I am a herdsman, slips me by,
Nor stays to hear how to the mountain-glens
Fair Dionysus did a heifer drive,

Nor knows she how that with a shepherd-man
Cypris abode, and in the Phrygian hills
Tended his flocks; how even Adonis' self
She loved in oakwoods, and in oakwoods mourned.
Who was Endymion? tell me; was he not
A herdsman?—yes—and as he kept his herds
Selené loved him.　From Olympus' top
Down to the Latmian vale she stooped, and came
Alone to couch beside her blooming boy.
Thou also, Rhea, dost weep thy herdsman lost;
And thou, great son of Chronos, didst not thou
Hover on pinions round a shepherd-maid?
One only does not love the herd-tending swain,
Eunica only; greater she forsooth
Than Cybelé, Selené; greater she
Than Cypris;—well then, Cypris, never more
Or in the city, or among the hills,
Make bold to love thy Ares, and at night
Fail not to press a solitary couch.

IDYL XXI.

𝕿𝖍𝖊 𝕱𝖎𝖘𝖍𝖊𝖗𝖘.

———

But one thing, Diophantus, stirs up skill,
But one thing schools to labour—poverty ;
Whose boding cares permit the toiling hind
Not even to slumber ; if for one short hour
Of night he hover on the land of sleep,
Sudden the thronging troubles rise amain,
And scare repose.

            It chanced that two old men,
Two fishers, shared the selfsame couch. Beneath
Their hut of woven osier they had strewn
Some withered sea-weed, and against the wall,
A wall of leaves, they rested. Close beside
There lay the weapons of their handicraft,—
Baskets, and rods, and hooks, and oozy nets,
Tackle of horse-hair, fleeces, creels, and lines,
Meshes of rush, and over sunken reefs

An old skiff anchored; and below their head
A little mat, rough raiment, and head-gear.
The fishers' work was here, and this their wealth.
Nor door nor dog was in their house,—all such
Seemed to them out of place; for poverty
Clave to them; other neighbour in their midst
Was none; but evermore on either side
The sea washed softly by the narrow hut.
Not yet the chariot of the moon had run
Its halfway course, when to their wonted toil
The fishers woke, and shaking sleep away
From sleepy lids upraised a mutual strain.

ASPHALION.

They lie, good friend, who say that summer nights
Are shorter, when the god sends length of days.
Already have I dreamed a thousand dreams,
Yet not a glimpse of dawn!   Am I deceived,
Or what? for sure the nights wane tardily.

COMPANION.

You blame, Asphalion, the sweet summer-time,
But wrongly; for no season of itself
Outlives its course; but care cuts off our sleep,
And makes the night seem long.

ASPHALION.

                    Didst ever learn
To read the visions of the night?   I've seen
Such fine ones.   And I would not own a *dream*
Unshared by you: in fishing we go halves,

And we'll go halves in rights of fantasy.
He that can solve a riddle with his wit
Is his own teacher and the best of seers.
Besides, we've lots of time.   Who could do what
Lying on a bed of leaves beside the sea,
And sleeping, if he sleep, with no delight
For thorns and thistles?   Light?   well, there's a lamp
In the townhall; and that's their business
To keep it going.

COMPANION.

                              Come, this midnight vision
Disclose, and let your comrade know the whole.

ASPHALION.

Last evening I was dozing in the midst
Of hooks and lines, and not from too much food,—
For, as you recollect, we supped betimes,
And spared our stomachs.   Well, I saw myself
Upon a rock, all eager for success.
I sat and watched the fishes, while the bait
I dangled temptingly.   Of a sudden, one
Of the biggest seized it—(so it is in sleep;
Hounds vision monstrous bears, I monstrous fish).
He stuck about the hook till blood 'gan flow,
And with his struggling all the rod was bent.
Tightening my hands, I found no easy task
To land the monster with such feeble gear;
Till, mindful of his wound, I lightly struck,
And gave him line; and when he ran no more,

I held him tight.   Seeing the fight was done,
I pulled him up,—a golden fish! all gold,
All over him.   And I stood fixed in fear
That he were something by Poseidon loved,
Or gray-green Amphitrité's treasured fish.
I loosed him lightly from the hook, that so
No gold be torn from off his mouth, and dragged
My boat ashore with ropes, and vowed a vow
Never again to set a foot on sea,
But stay on shore, and lord it with my gold.
And this awoke me.   Now, friend, for the rest
Apply your wit to solve it; as for me,
I tremble at the oath I undertook.

COMPANION.

You need not tremble, for you never swore.
The golden fish you saw you never found.
Such sights as these are nothing more than lies.
If in real truth you go when wide awake
To test hopes born of sleep, and search the sea,
Look for a fish of flesh; or else belike
You'll die of hunger, though you dream of gold.

IDYL XXII.

The Dioscuri.

————

SING we the sons of ægis-bearing Zeus
And Leda, Castor, and the dreadful strength
Of Polydeuces in the fight of fists,
With both hands braced about by leather thongs.
Twice and three times sing we the stalwart sons
Of Thestius' daughter, the twin brethren lords
Of Lacedæmon, that are near to help
Men on the edge of ruin, steeds distrest
In crush of gory war, and ships forlorn
That struggling against adverse signs of heaven
Setting and rising, meet with stormy winds
That raise a mighty billow in their rear,
Or by the prow, or from what point they will,
And hurl it on the bark, and stave its sides;
Rigging and sails hang loosely, torn and slashed
At random; and a heavy rain from heaven

Steals on at night, and smitten with hard hail,
And lashed by winds, the ocean wide resounds.
Yet for all that ev'n from the dread abyss,
With all her sailors that had looked to die,
Ye draw the ship ; instant the winds are lulled,
Soft calm is o'er the surface of the deep,
Hither and thither course the broken clouds,
Shine forth the Bears, faintly in Cancer's midst
Glimmers the shadowy manger of the Ass,
And all things speak a favourable voyage.
O, friends in need to mortals, loved ones both,
Horsemen, harp-players, athletes, sons of song !
Which shall be first ? shall Castor be my theme,
Or Polydeuces ?   Both are on my tongue ;
But Polydeuces shall be hymned the first.

    Now had ship Argo, from the rocks escaped
That clash together, and the ominous gulfs
Of wintry Pontus, borne the heavenly pair
Unto the Bebrycans ; from either side
Down by the ladder stepped full many a chief
From Jason's ship, and on a breadth of beach,
A wind-swept strand, they landed ; there they piled
Their couches, and struck tinder into sparks.
Far from their comrades roamed the godlike pair,
Horse-taming Castor, Polydeuces swart,
Scouring the savage thickets on the hill.
Under a smooth sheer cliff they found a spring,
An everflowing well of taintless lymph,
And every pebble sparkled underneath

Like crystal or like silver ; and around
Grew towering pines and crested cypresses,
Platans, and poplars white, and odorous blooms
That burst upon the fields in waning spring,
The happy labours of the downy bees.
There sat a mighty man the livelong day,—
A man of dreadful aspect, for his ears
Were crushed and battered by hard fists ; his chest
Swelled hugely, and his broadened back, with flesh
Of iron, like a statue hammer-wrought ;
Stood up the muscles on his brawny arms
Under the shoulder, like great boulder-stones
Whirled by a wintry torrent, and worn smooth
In many an eddy ; and around his neck
Over his back there hung a lion's hide
Tied by the paws.   Him first of all addressed
Polydeuces, in the athlete fights renowned.

POLYDEUCES.

Health, whosoever thou art.   Who are they that in-
    habit this region ?

AMYCUS.

How have I health in beholding men whom I never set
    eyes on ?

POLYDEUCES.

Fear not ; trust me thou seest not robbers, or scions of
    robbers.

AMYCUS.

I am not given to fear ; nor from thee shall I learn my
    lessons.

POLYDEUCES.

Savage thou art, overweening, thy temper in all things
　　malignant.

AMYCUS.

Such as I am thou dost see me.　I stand not on land
　　of thy owning.

POLYDEUCES.

Come if thou wilt, be my guest, and return to thy home
　　gift-laden.

AMYCUS.

None of thy gifts for me ;—and mine do not chance to
　　be handy.

POLYDEUCES.

Surely, good man, thou wilt never refuse me a draught
　　of this water?

AMYCUS.

Thou shalt find out, so soon as with thirst thy dry lips
　　are shrivelled.

POLYDEUCES.

Say, can we offer in recompense silver, or aught to per-
　　suade thee?

AMYCUS.

One against one lift hands, stand up face to face with
　　a fighter.

POLYDEUCES.

Face to face shall the fight be with fists, or shall feet
　　join in struggle?

AMYCUS.

Fight with the outstretched fist, and spare not from
  showing thy science.

POLYDEUCES.

Where is the man against whom I must bind my hands
  with the cæstus?

AMYCUS.

Here is the man, close by; not reckoned a baby at
  boxing.

POLYDEUCES.

Is there a prize prepared, for which we may join in the
  combat?

AMYCUS.

I will be thine, as thou shalt be mine if I turn out the
  victor.

POLYDEUCES.

This is the way that cocks crimson-crested settle their
  battles.

AMYCUS.

Whether or not either cocks or lions fight in this fashion,
This and none other for thee and me shall be prize of
  battle.

Spake Amycus, and lifting up his horn
Wound a shrill blast, at echo of whose notes
Under the shady platans came in haste,
Troop after troop, the long-haired Bebrycans.
Nor less the lord of battle, Castor, sped
To summon forth from the Magnesian bark

The heroes all.   And now the mighty pair
Armour of leathern coils about their hands,
Long folds of bracing wreathed around their limbs,
Were midway led, breathing out blood and death
Each at the other.   Instant was a strife,
Great was the struggle which should gain best ground
And catch the summer sun upon his back.
But, Polydeuces, thou didst far surpass
Thy bulky foe in craft; and the full face
Of Amycus was smitten by the rays.
Then waxed he wroth, and launching out his fists
Came on; but Polydeuces, as he came,
Struck full upon his chin, and stirred his rage
Beyond all bounds; rushed he to force the fight,
Hurling his weight with head to earth inclined.
Shouted the Bebrycans, and in refrain
The hero-band cheered Polydeuces on,
Fearing by chance this man of Tityan might
In a narrow pass should press and pin him down.
But shifting here and there the son of Zeus
Struck with each hand alternate, and stalled off,
Fierce as it was, the rush of Amycus.
He with the blows stood reeling, clots of gore
Out-spirting; and one mighty shout arose
From all the braves seeing his cheeks and mouth
Defaced with wounds and bruises, and his eyes
Shrunk up amid the lumps of swollen flesh.
With many a feint and vain delivery—
Now here, now there—the hero harassed him,

Till that he saw him helpless, then struck high
Betwixt his eyebrows full upon his nose,
Baring his face to the bone. Back from the blow
He stretched his length among the summer leaves.
But when he rose the fight waxed fierce again,
Heavy on each fell thuds of leathern thongs.
One at the chest took aim, the Bebrycan ;
Wide of the neck he struck : but Polydeuces,
Victor unvanquished, heaped defacing blows,
Till face was undistinguishable pulp.
Flesh was nigh vanishing away in sweat ;
He that was great became a little man
In little time ; while with each touch of toil
Ever the son of Zeus had mightier thews,
And fairer to behold his countenance.

How Polydeuces crushed this glutton bulk,
Say, goddess, for thou knowest ; I but speak
At secondhand the words of other men,
As thou dost bid me, and as thou wouldst have.

Yet yearning to perform some doughty deed
Rose Amycus, and gripped with his left hand
The left hand of his foe, bending across
To 'scape the attack, and sudden with his right
Swung from his side a brawny arm. Perchance
Then had he maimed the Amyclæan king ;
But Polydeuces slipped his head aside,
And with clenched fist on the left temple struck,
And threw his whole weight on him ; and anon
Spirted the black blood from his gaping brow.

Then with his left he hit him on the mouth,
Till every tooth loud rattled, and again
The blows rang fast and faster, till his face
Was battered, his cheeks smashed, and down to earth
All of a heap he fell, beside himself,
And stretched his hands out, to renounce the strife,
Seeing that he was very nigh to death.
Then Polydeuces, victor as thou wert,
Thou didst take no mean triumph ; and he swore
A mighty oath, invoking from the sea
His sire Poseidon, never more again
To vex and trouble strangers wittingly.

　　　Thus have I hymned thee, king; now, Castor, thee,
Thee will I sing, O son of Tyndarus,
Lord of swift steeds, spear-shaker, sheathed in brass.

　　　Now the twin sons of Zeus had borne away
Two daughters of Leucippus ; and anon
Followed in hot chase their affianced lords,
Lynceus and stalwart Idas, brethren two,
The sons of Aphareus ; but when they neared
The tomb of their dead sire, all at once
Leapt from their cars, and stood forth in array,
Heavy with pond'rous spears and orbèd shields.
Under his helm loud echoed Lynceus' voice :

　　　" Warriors, why seek ye battle? why molest
The brides of others ? wherefore in your hands
Glitters the naked steel ?　Surely to us,
Far, far before all other men to us
Leucippus pledged his daughters, and an oath

Strengthened our marriage-pact; but ye with gifts,
Oxen and mules and lowing herds and flocks,
Have basely won him o'er to rival suits,
And stolen our wives from us by bribery.
Often and often to your face I said,
I not a man of words, yet many a time
I said to both : 'Beseems not thus, good friends,
For princes to woo wives whose plighted faith
Is given already unto future lords.
There is wide Sparta, Elis trod by steeds,
There is Arcadia with its myriad flocks,
Argos, Messené, and the Achæan states,
And all the length of the Sisyphian strand :
There in their native homes are nurturèd
Ten thousand maidens with no fault of face,
No lack of beauty, and no want of mind,
Easy for you to have your will of these,
And mate at pleasure ; many a sire exults
In valiant sons-in-law ; and ye stand out
Above all other heroes, ye, your sires,
And upward through the whole ancestral line.
Suffer, then, friends, the issue of our bond ;
And for yourselves, be it our common task
To find some other marriage.'
                         "This I said,
This and much more ; into the ocean wave
The wind swept all my words, my speech obtained
No grace : seeing ye are inexorable,
And harsh of temper.   Yet even now give way :

L

Ye are our kinsmen on the mother's side.
But if your hearts are yearning for the war,
And blood must stain our spears, and mutual strife
Burst forth, Idas and Polydeuces brave,
His kinsman, from the combat shall retire,
And hold their hands from fighting. But we two,
Castor and I, the younger of the pairs,
Will try the war. So be our parents spared
Too heavy woe. Sufficient for one house
A single corpse ; and they two that remain,
Bridegrooms instead of corpses, shall give joy
To all their comrades, and shall wed these maids :
So shall great strife be cancelled with small harm."

So said he ; and the god gave not his words
To empty winds : therefore the elder pair
Unbraced their arms, and laid them on the ground,
And Lynceus stood, shaking his forceful spear,
Fenced by his orbèd shield ; nor Castor less
Poised his sharp lance ; nodded their horsehair plumes :
With many a jav'lin-thrust they laboured first,
Each striving if he haply might descry
Some undefended spot ; but rooted deep
I' the massy bucklers the lance-heads broke off
Ere either gat a hurt ; then from the sheaths
Drawing their swords they rushed with murderous
    thought
Each against each : the battle knew no rest.
Oft at the wide-spread shield and crested helm
Struck Castor, oft keen-sighted Lynceus smote

His foeman's buckler, and his sharp sword swept
High as the crimson plumes ; until at length
He cut at the left knee, and Castor sprang
Suddenly to the left, and smote his hand,
And shore it off; he, stricken grievously,
Let fall his sword, and turned in headlong flight
Towards his father's tomb, where Idas lay
And gazed upon the war of kith and kin.
But rushing on the son of Tyndarus
Right through his flank and navel thrust his blade,
And cleft his entrails.   There upon the ground
Bent Lynceus, and the heavy sleep of death
Pressed on his eyes.
              Nor at his father's hearth
Laocoösa e'er again beheld
His brother, or prepared his marriage-feast.
For tearing from the tomb of Apharcus
A column of support that rose thereby,
Fain was Messenian Idas with all haste
To hurl his brother's slayer to the earth ;
But Zeus was nigh to help in time of need,
And dashed the chiselled marble from his hands,
And scorched him with his flaming bolts of fire.
So with the sons of Tyndarus to war
Is no light matter.   They are men of might,
And mighty is the author of their race.
    Children of Leda, hail, and evermore
Bid fame attend my hymns.   All sons of song
Are dear to you, the sons of Tyndarus,

To Helen, and to all the hero chiefs
That armed for Menelaüs, and achieved
The wreck of Ilium.   For you, O kings,
The Chian bard has wrought eternal fame,
Singing of Priam's city, and the ships
Of Greece, the battles on the plains of Troy,
And great Achilles, bulwark of the war.
I too for you bring honied melodies,
Such as they are, the clear-voiced Muses' gifts,
As they inspire me, and my strength permits.
Song to the gods is sweetest sacrifice.

IDYL XXIV.

ALCMENA, she of Midea, took one day
The ten-months Hercules, and Iphicles,
His junior by a night, and washed them both,
And plenished them with milk, and laid them down
Within the hollow of a brazen shield,
Which erst Amphitryon stripped, a goodly arm,
From fallen Pterelaüs.   On their heads
She gently laid her hands, and whispered low :
    " Sleep, infants, sweetly sleep, and wake again ;
Sleep, sleep, my life, two brothers, safe and sound ;
Sleep happy there, and happy greet the morn !"
    So saying, she rocked the massy shield, and soon
Sleep held them fast.   But at the midnight hour,
What time the Bear is sunken to his wane,
And near Orion bulges into light
A monstrous shoulder,—then two awful forms,

Serpents with shuddery sweep of night-black coils,
Heré, untired in artful wiles, despatched
Towards the broad threshold, where the hollow posts
Support the palace-gates, urging them on
To feast upon the infant Hercules.

So glode they on their bellies along the ground
Greedy for blood ; a gleam of devilish fire
Shone in their coming eyes, and venomous drops
They spirted blightingly.   But when their tongue
Played round the children (close as that they were),—
Just then, so Zeus divinely ordered all,
Uprose Alcmena's babes ; and, lo, the house
Was filled with light.   One of them, Iphicles,
Over the hollow shield when he perceived
The evil brutes, and saw the insatiate fangs,
Called lustily, and gat him up to flee,
Kicking the fleecy blanket with his feet.
Him with restraining hands did Hercules
Hold back ; then with most strenuous gripe he
          squeezed
And kept those two screwed down, clutched by the
          gorge,
Wherein are hid the baneful poison-cells
Of damnèd snakes, whom even gods abhor.
And round about the late-born child, unweaned,
And tearless e'en in infancy, they wound
Themselves in folds, and back again unwound,
Forbye their necks were anguished, and they fain
Would find solution of such fateful grip.

Alcmena heard the cry, and rose at once.
" Up, up, Amphitryon, for a grievous fear
Fastens upon me ; up, nor stay to dress
Thy feet in sandals.   Hearest not the shouts
O' the younger child ? and art not thou aware
That somehow in the dead of night these walls
Are all ablaze with brilliance ? though as yet
Is no clear sparkle of aurorean light :
Something unwelcome, strange, is in the house,
Dearest of men."   She said, and from the couch
He leapt obedient to the entreating wife,
Grasped at his embossed sword, that alway hung
High on a hook above the cedarn bed ;
With one hand to the new-spun belt he reached,
And with the other lifted the huge sheath,
A figured work.   But, lo, the wide-spread room
Was filled again with darkness and black night.
    Then called he to the heavy-snoring slaves :
" Up, slaves ! and quick as thought go rake the hearth
For fire, and bring it here, and haste to close
And bar the stubborn fastenings of the doors.
Up, slaves stout-hearted ! 'tis your master calls."
    Then quickly thronged the slaves with lamps ablaze,
And every one made haste, and all the house
Was filled.   But when they saw the suckling child,
Their Hercules, and in his tender hands
Two monstrous beasts gripped tightly,—lo, they clapped
Their palms together, and they cried aloud.
He to Amphitryon his father showed

The reptiles, and with lofty leaps of joy
Made mirth of all, and at his father's feet
Offering with smiles the huge mis-shapen bulks,
Laid them, all heavy with the weight of death.
    Then to her bosom fair Alcmena took
Iphicles, sore distressed, and lean with fear ;
And underneath his lambswool coverlid
Amphitryon laid the other, and strode back
To his chamber, not unmindful of sweet sleep.
But when the frequent carollings of birds
Sang out the twilight, lo, Alcmena called
The seer Tiresias, teller of all truth,
And spoke the new occasion of her need,
And bade him answer how these things should be.
" Fear not to reveal whate'er the gods intend,
Be it of evil.   Should I lesson thee,
Everes' prophet-son, who knowest too well
How vain for man to shun what ills soe'er
Fate with untiring spindle hurries on ?"
    So said the queen.   To whom the seer replied :
" Mother of a famous race, inheritress
Of Perseus' blood, take heart.   Of what must be,
'Tis better far to enshrine the better part
Within thy mind.   Listen, and hear me swear
By that so precious light that long ago
Has faded from my eyes,—the time shall come
When many a dame of this Achæan land,
Teasing the tender threads about her knee
Into a woof, shall sing Alcmena's name

At eventide; and thou shalt be revered
By Argive women.   Such an one is he,
This son of thine, that shall in future time
Climb the star-studded heaven, from the breast
A broadly-moulded hero, much above
All mortal men, and wild innumerous beasts.
Twelve labours must he work, and then doth fate
Will him to rest within the dome of Zeus;
And all of mortal the Trachinian pyre
Shall have.   He shall be owned as kith and kin
Of the immortals, who have goaded on
These monster-snakes, lurking to tear piecemeal
His infant limbs.   Truly a day shall come
Wherein the wolf, spying the couchant fawn,
Shall spare to rend him with his jagged teeth.
Now therefore, woman, see that fire be waked
Among the ashes, and look out dry logs,
Rosewood, or thorn, or brambles of the copse,
Or withering wild-pear blasted by the winds,
And in the fierce flame of that kindling brush
Burn the two serpents at the midnight hour,
What time they hungered to destroy thy child.
And in the morning let some serving-man
Collect the ashes, carry them away,
And hurl them o'er the confines of the land,
Across the river to the rifted rocks,
And back return with unreverted face.
But first beware to incense all the house
With virgin sulphur; then, as custom is,

Sprinkle the waters of a taintless stream
Sharpened with salt, and with an olive-shoot
Dash the libation, and to Zeus above
Let bleed a porker, so that ye may rise
Superior to the strength of baneful powers."
Thus spoke Tiresias, and turned to leave,
Much burdened with the weight of many years,
And set himself to ascend his ivory car.

    Then, like a young plant in some garden-ground,
His mother nurtured Hercules, the child
In semblance of Argive Amphitryon.
Learned he his letters of Apollo's son,
Old Linus, stalwart, ever-wakeful guard ;
And to expand the bow, and rightly aim
The feathered reeds, he learned of Eurytus,
Rich-dowered with bounty of ancestral lands.
Another music taught,—Eumolpus he,
Philammon's son, and on the boxwood lyre
Steadied and shaped his fingers ; and all else—
What trips and shifts the Argos wrestlers try,
Cross-buttocks, play of intertwinèd limbs,
And how the fiercer athlete plies the fight
With cæstuses ; and how when fallen to earth,
Armed at all points, their lissome writhings twine,
By skill, not chance, involved,—all this he learned
Of Hermes, under guidance of a youth,
Harpalycus of Phanoté, of whom
Once seen, how far soever, in the strife
Contesting, rare was he that dared abide

The onset,—such a gloom of lowering brows
Hung o'er his awful face. And how to rein
The coursers from his car, and round the turn
Bend safely, that the axles take no harm,
Amphitryon taught his son with kind intent,
Since many a time from out the rushing race
In Argos, famed for horses, had he won
Much treasure, and his chariots still stood sound,
Unbroken, that had borne him, though for long
Slacked was the harness. Next to hurl the spear
In single conflict, by the sheltering shield
Protected, and abide the thrusting sword,
And train the phalanx, and dispose his troops
To attack the foe, and lead the sounding charge,
Horse-taming Castor taught him,—he who fled
From Argos, when Tydéan might possessed
All the wide land and all the vine-clad plains
That erst Adrastus held in Argolis,
The home of horses and horse-taming men;
And never, till old age had worn away
The edges of his youth, was such an one
Among the ranks of heroes, that could vie
With Castor in the clash of furious war.

So at his mother's will was Hercules
Fashioned and shaped; for him was spread a couch
Close to his father, strewn with lions' skins,
His joy and pride; and for his morning meal
The flesh of beeves quick-broiled, and in a crate
Of wicker-work a massive Dorian loaf,

Ample to satisfy a son of the soil.
And at the evening hour a little food
That had not seen the fire; and round his legs
He wore some unkempt coverings . . . .

   *   *   *   *   *

[*The rest is lost.*]

IDYL XXV.

The Lion of Nemea.

[*The beginning is lost.*]

*　　*　　*　　*　　*　　*

THEN answer made the aged husbandman,
Chief in the gardens, resting from his work,
That lay beside him : "All thou askest, friend,
Willingly will I answer ; for I fear
The wrath of wayside Hermes ;—he, they say,
Of all the heavenly ones is angered most
To see a traveller in eager search
Of aid in travel, and that aid denied.
Know, first of all, the herds and flocks long-haired
Of king Augeas are not pastured all
In the same meads or on one stretch of land ;
But some along the banks of Helison feed,
And some beside Alpheüs' holy stream,

And some around Buprasium, where the vines
Droop down grape-loaded, and some also here.
And sheltering homesteads are for all prepared
Distinctly ; and for all the innumerous hosts,
How vast soever, still the pastures bloom
With never-fading verdure, far away
To the mighty pool of Menius ; sweet the grass,
Fat bounty of the dew-bespangled fields,
Saturate with marshy moistness ;—sweet and strong
To swell the growing strength of hornèd kine.
Clearly upon the right thou mayst behold
Over the flowing river all the range
Of sleeping-places : there are groves of plane
Thick-leaved ; and there the pale wild-olive grows,
Beside the temple of the pastoral god
Apollo, great fulfiller of desires.
And straight along is many a lengthened line
Of quarters builded for us country-folk,
Who labour out with zeal huge store of wealth
For him our king, sowing from time to time
The thrice-ploughed fallows, ay and four times too.
Each planter knows his station ; and when days
Of seasonable warmth arrive, they turn
To other toils, the labour of the vats.
All that thou seest is lorded o'er by one
Augeas, bounteous king ; and all the plain,
Wheat-bearing lands, and orchards dense with trees,
E'en to the uttermost rock that overtops
The many-fountained uplands. All day long

Labouring we traverse them; such lot befals
Us servants, that our life is in the fields.
But tell me (so the purpose of thy mind
May be advantaged), whether need of aught
Has brought thee hither;—dost thou seek to see
Augeas, or who on the king attend,
One of his household? Surely, if I knew,
I would speak plainly; for I dare be sworn
Thou art of no base birth, nor hast thyself
Semblance of baseness, so thy mighty form
Stands out surpassing, that I well might deem
The sons of the immortals, who abide
With mortal men, are fashioned such as thou."

To him the valiant son of Zeus replied:
" Yes, I would see the Epeian king, old man,
Augeas; need of him has led me here.
But if he be within the city walls
Among his townsmen, for the public weal
Intent, and rival claims to adjudge aright,
Bid some attendant come and lead the way;
Some hind above the rest preferred, to whom
I may unfold my tale, and he to me
Impart in turn : so has God fashioned man
To lean upon his fellow." Then forthwith
Hasted to speak the worthy husbandman :

" Friend, not uncounselled by some heavenly power
Hast thou come hither : so, with no delay
All that thou dost desire shall be fulfilled.
For yesterday the son of Helios,

Augeas, and his stalwart high-born heir
Phyleus, came from the city to survey
For many a day the boundless heritage
That crowds these lands : haply when kings themselves
Take active guardianship, they deem their state
Is safer. Let us go. I to my cote
Will lead the way, so we may find the king."

So saying, he walked before him ; pondering much
About the stranger, whence he could have come,
With such a wild-beast's skin, and such a club,
A mighty handful : ever on the point
To ask ; but ever as the rising word
Hung on his lip, he swallowed it in fear,
Lest some untimely utterance should offend.
Hard is it to divine another's mind.
Far off of their approach the dogs were ware,
Scented their skins, and heard their tramping feet :
With deafening din they rushed from every side
At Hercules, Amphitryon's son ; and yelped
At the other idly, yelped and fawned at once.
He from the ground in haste picked store of stones,
Scared them to pell-mell flight, and rated all
With threatening voice, and stopped their clamorous
tongues,
But glad that though himself were far away
They watched the tent, he shaped his thought in
words :
" Well, what a thing is this the sovereign gods
Have given to live with man ! how full of care !

Could it but reason with itself and know
Whom to be wrath against, when to refrain,
No other beast could then compare for worth :
Now is it very fierce, and all untamed."
    He said, and striding on with hasty steps
Anon they reached the threshold. Helios now
Had turned his horses toward the fields of gloom,
Driving the westering day : to folds and pens
Home from the field the well-fed flocks returned.
Then one after another hove in view
Thousand on thousand oxen, like rain-clouds
Driven along in heaven by the might
Of Notus or the Thracian boreal blast,
Whose number none can tell, so swift they scud
Through æther, nor their ending ; for the wind
Mightily rolls them onward to the front,
And one upon another surges up.
So oxen after oxen from behind
Streamed to the stalls : and all the plain was filled,
And all the roadways with the advancing herds ;
And all the wide-spread acres rang to the full
With bellowings ; quickly then the stalls received
The rolling mass of heavy-footed kine,
And in the yards the sheep were folded safe.
Then none of all the countless servitors
Stood still, but one with well-cut thongs confined
The milch-cows' feet, and stood beside and milked ;
Another brought the young ones to their dams,
Eager to drain the pleasant nourishment.

One stood and held a milking-pail, and one
Curdled a fat rich cheese ; and one within
Led off the bulls from consort with their mates.
And in and out the stables peered the king
Augeas, how the herdsmen kept their charge
Observant ; with him, as he passed in view
His huge possessions, met in the way his son,
And towering strength of high-souled Hercules.
He, though of dauntless and unbroken heart,
Ready for all occasions, stood and stared
In blank amazement at the countless swarm
Of oxen.   Where was he that dare assert
Or hazard the idea that such array
Was one man's birthright—one, or ten besides,
Ten kings, the richest of flock-owning chiefs?
But Helios to his son had given, that he
Should far surpass all others in the wealth
Of flocks and herds ; and them for ever and aye
He kept increasing ; never fell disease
Attacked his homesteads, such as brings to naught
The herdsman's labour : ever more and more
Numbered his hornèd cattle, year by year
Better and stronger ; bringing forth alive
Their countless young, a female progeny.
Three hundred bulls among them stalked about,
White-legged, with twisting horns ; two hundred more
Of blood-red hue ;—all useful at the stud.
And twelve besides were tended in the fields,
Sacred to Helios : swan-like was their skin,

Bright white ; above all swaying-footed things
Preëminent ; they roaming by themselves
Cropped the rich verdurous herbage, in their strength
Hugely exulting : when the swift wild beast,
Leaving his bushy covert sallies out
Into the plain to seize the pasturing kine,
These first rush on, and scent the coming war
With fearful lowings, and a face that glares
Death and destruction.   First of these in might
And muscle and high-mettled valorousness
Was Phaëthon the great ; whom herdsmen all
Likened to some bright star ; since many a time,
Roaming with other oxen, from afar
He sparkled, and his form seemed full of light.
He, when he saw the tawny lion's skin,
Now withered, straight at watchful Hercules
Rushed in a furious bound, with bended head,
And stubborn front aimed firmly at his chest.
Him in his course the hero's mighty arm
Stayed, by the left horn clutched ; down to the
                          earth
He bore his neck, all brawny as it was ;
And pushed him back and pressed him heavily
With straining shoulder, till the muscle swelled
Around his sinews, and above his arm
Stood up erect.   Amazement held the king,
Phyleus his valiant son, and all the hinds
Beside the long-horned cattle, when they saw
The overwhelming might of Hercules.

Then to the city, leaving far behind
The fertile pastures, walked in company
Phyleus and Hercules.　But when they reached
The margin of the people-bearing road,
Measuring with hasty feet the narrow track
That wound among the vineyards from the stalls,
Scarce seen, not easy to be followed up
For faintness in the dense continuous wood;
Then him that was behind, the progeny
Of highest Zeus, Augeas' son addressed,
Turning his head a little to the right
Over his shoulder : "Long ago, methinks,
O stranger, have I heard great talk of thee,
So my heart tells me; for there came a man
From Argos, in the spring-tide of his youth,
Achæan, from the shore of Helicé.
He, in the frequence of the Epeian peers
Told us that under witness of himself
An Argive man had slain a horrid beast,
An awful lion, most disastrous plague
To all the country folk, whose hollow lair
Was close beside the grove of Nemean Zeus.
Whether from holy Argos of a truth
I could not certify.　He might have dwelt
In Tiryns or Mycenæ : so he said;
But added (if my memory serve me right)
That Perseus was the fountain of his race.
Sure am I none but thou could dare such deed
Of all the Achæans ;—clearly this proclaims

The wild-beast's skin, labour of vast emprise,
That clothes thy limbs.   Tell me then, first of all,
That I may know, great hero, if my mind
Presages right or wrong ;—say, art thou he
With whom the Achæan filled our listening ears,
And do I guess thee rightly ?—say beside
How of thyself thou venturedst to destroy
This beast, and how it came to invade the plains
Of Nemea the well-watered ; such a pest,
How great soe'er thy wish, thou couldst not find
Throughout Achæa ; for it nurtures not
Such mighty bulks, but rather bears, and swine,
And many a noxious tribe of ravening wolves.
Therefore they wondered much that heard the tale :
'Twas but a traveller's lies, so some maintained,
Tickling the crowd with empty mouthing talk."

      So saying, from the middle road aside
Stepped Phyleus, that the way might be enough
For both together,—he the better hear
The words of Hercules, who, closing up,
Thus launched his story : "What thou askedst first,
Son of Augeas, hast thyself with ease
Divinèd rightly : but about this beast
Since thou art fain to hear, I will tell all,
And how the thing was done ;—saving alone
The place he came from ; *that* not all the men
Of all the Argive cities could declare.
Only we fancy that some heavenly power,
In vengeance for neglected sacrifice,

Let loose this scourge upon Phoroneus' land.
For, like a river, sweeping all away,
Came down upon the dwellers of the plain
A lion, mercilessly ravaging them,
And most of all who dwelt beside his haunt,
The Bembinæans, fared intolerably.
This, the first trial set me to fulfil,
Eurystheus ordered, that the fateful beast
Should die by me.   Straightway I gat me forth,
Taking my pliant bow, and quiver stocked
With arrows; in the other hand my club,
Massive, unpeeled, unemptied of its pith,
A wild-olive creviced in a toppling crag,
That once upon the slope of Helicon
I found, and tore it up, thick roots and all.
But, when I came to where the lion lay,
I took my bow, and to the hookèd tip
Fitted the string, hurriedly laid across
The sorrow-storèd reed, and all around
I turned my eyes, straining to spy him out
Ere the destroyer could catch sight of me.
And now the noontide hour had come, and yet
I could discern no track and hear no roar;
No mortal in the new-sown furrow showed,
With oxen or at work, to aid my quest;
Such deathly fear kept everyone confined
Within their huts: still stayed I not my feet,
Scouring the heavy-foliaged mountain-sides
Until I saw him.   Now must instant proof

Decide my valour. At the near approach
Of evening he was stalking to his den,
Glutted with flesh and gore ; large gouts of blood
Befouled his bristly jaws and visage grim
And chest; and with his tongue he licked his beard.
Far off upon a wooded height I lay
Shrouded in shady foliage, fixed to await
His coming.   Instant as he issued forth,
An arrow sped and struck on his left flank ;
How vainly! never the point could pierce his flesh,
But back rebounded to the sallow grass.
Then quickly from the ground in wonderment
He reared his head ; everywhere ran his eyes
Flaming around him ; and a gaping grin
Disclosed his gluttonous fangs.   Much uncontent
That all for naught the first had fled my hand,
I launched a second arrow from the string,
And struck him in the midriff, where the lungs
Are situate ; and again the bitter reed
Not even pierced his hide, but back to earth
Dropped in like manner harmless at his feet.
Then was I instant, raging inwardly,
To draw a third ; but, glaring all around,
The ruthless beast beheld me ; round his legs
He lashed his mighty tail, and in his heart
Bethought him of the battle ; all his neck
Was swoln with passion, and his tawny mane
Stiffened to bristle, as he snarled in rage :
Stood up his backbone like a bended bow,

And every part of him, about his flanks,
And round about his loin, was bulged and bent.
  So fares it with some chariot-making man,
Skilled in his business, when a sapling shoot,
Cut from a fissile fig-tree of the woods,
He takes and bends, heating it in the fire
Till fitted for a chariot axle-nave;
Sudden from out his hand the branch escapes
Of fig thick-rinded; with a single bound
It flies on high.   So leapt at me from afar
The savage lion, hurled himself in a mass,
Hungry to tear my flesh.   I with one hand
Held out my arrows, and let droop my robe
Twice-folded from the shoulder; overhead
With the other hand I raised my seasoned club
And smote him on the temple; right in twain
Shivered the tough wild-olive on his skull,
Shaggy, unvanquished yet; and down he fell,
Or ever he reached me, from mid-air to earth.
There stood he with feet quivering,—his head
Swooned to and fro, and over both his eyes
A dimming darkness floated, and his brain
Reeled with the shatter of his skull.   Anon,
Seeing him anguished, all beside himself
With grievous pain, I rushed to force the fight,
Ere he could rally with returning strength.
I threw my bow away upon the ground
And woven quiver; and about his neck
I beat him, on the nape, and throttled him

Most masterfully, gripping from behind
With brawny hands, that so my flesh might 'scape
His tearing talons. Steadily I pressed
With both my heels his hindmost feet to earth,
Weighing upon his quarters; and my ribs
Kept down his swelling thighs, until at length
I loosed my arms, and lifted him on high,
A breathless bulk, and to the drear abode
Of Hades fled the monster's mighty soul.
Then took I counsel how to strip away
From off the dead beast's limbs the bristly hide—
A grievous labour; for at all attempts
Nor steel, nor stone, nor wood had any power
To sever it. But some immortal God
Gave me this notion, that his very claws
Would tear his skin. Quickly I stripped it off
 With them; and girt it round about my limbs
To shield me in the furious blood-stained rout
Of battle. Perished thus the Nemean beast,
Erewhile a grievous scourge to flocks and men."

IDYL XXIX.

The Lover's Complaint.*

TRUTH, my lover, they say in wine abideth;
We have drunk, and let us be truthful also.
Hear, then, all that within my breast lies hidden.
Thou art loth with a perfect heart to love me;
Well I know, for but half my life remaineth,
Thou art here in thy charms, all else is vanished.
When thou willest, I live like gods in heaven;
When thou willest it not, I grope in darkness.
Is it right that a lover thus be tortured?
List to me, I am older, thou art younger;
Thou wilt happier be, and praise my counsel:
Build high up in the boughs of one tree one nest,
Where may never a noisome reptile clamber.
Now to-day upon this branch here thy home is,
There to-morrow; from tree to tree thou roamest.
Whoso looks on thy face and marks thy beauty,

---

* The glyconic metre of the original is not conveniently
reproducible in English. I have therefore treated it hendeca-
syllabically.

Him as more than a three-years friend thou hailest,
While thou holdest a first fond love as nothing.
Thou dost swell, as of mighty matter moulded ;
Ah no ! love to the end a liker nature.
Then thy name shall be high through all the city ;
Love himself on thy life shall lie not heavy ;
Love that easily tames the hearts of all men ;
Love that maketh me soft, who once was iron.
Now thy delicate lips I press so tightly :
O remember that last year thou wert younger ;
Ere thou spurn me, remember age is coming,
Wrinkled age ; nor can one recall his young years,
Never more ;—on his shoulders youth has wide wings,
We so slow that we cannot stay their flying.
Think of this, it were well ; be gentler-minded ;
Hear my prayer for a life of faithful loving ;
So that when on thy cheek comes down of manhood,
We may live like Achilles and Patroclus.
If my words to the whirling winds thou givest,
In thy heart saying, " Good man, why molest me ?"
Now for thee to the grove of golden apples,
Now to Cerberus hell's guard I would wander :
Then, not e'en wert thou calling at my house-door,
Would I move, for the fierce love would be ended.

IDYLS OF MOSCHUS.

IDYL I.

The Runaway.

CYPRIS was looking far and wide for Eros,
Her son : "If any spies him wandering
Where three ways meet, it is my runaway :
Who brings the news shall have the prize ; his wage
Cypris's kiss,—no empty kiss for *thee*
Who bringest him home ; but *thou*, friend, shalt have
    more.
He is a child of mark : thou wilt not fail
To know him among twenty.   Listen well !
The colour of his skin is never white,
But touched with living flame : his little eyes
Do blaze most piercingly : his speech is soft,
But wicked is his wit—at variance all
His thoughts and words : his voice is honey-sweet,
But when in wrath his mood is most ungentle,
Scorning the semblance and the guise of truth,
A crafty elf, whose very sport is fierce.
His forehead shines with clusters of fair curls ;

Ready for any devilry his face ;
And for his tiny little hands, they reach
Far down to Acheron and the king of the dead :
Naked his body, but the mind within
Is cloaked and shrouded—none can find it out.
And, like a bird, he flutters to and fro,
Here, there, from men to women, and on their hearts
Enthrones himself, holding a little bow,
And on the bow a dart—a little dart,
But strong to range from earth to highest heaven.
A golden quiver hangs upon his back ;
Within are shrined those bitter-barbèd reeds
That wound even *me*,—too often ! All is wild,
Untamed, about him—he, and all of his ;
And most of all that slender-flaming torch—
So small ! yet even Helios it fires.
If thou canst clutch him, bind him, pity him not ;
And if he weeps before thee, O beware,
Be not deluded !—if he laugh, hold fast :
But if he fain would kiss thee, fly for thy life !
His lips are poison, and his kiss is death !
And if he says, ' Lo, here are all my arms ;
I freely give them ; take them :'—touch them not ;
Deluding gifts, that have been steeped in fire."

IDYL II.

Europa.

Once to Europa came a pleasant dream
From Cypris, when the third watch of the night
Was now beginning, and the morn was near;
What time on tirèd eyelids sleep doth rest
Sweeter than honey, and with softest chain
Binds tirèd eyes, and every care is hushed,
And truthful visions flock around in crowds.
   Then, as she slept beneath the palace-roof,
Europa, child of Phœnix, still a maid,
Dreamed that two continents waged war for her,
Asia and Asia's opposite ;* who stood
In woman's form before her : one appeared
In shape and fashion of a foreign race;
The other, like a native of her land,
Ever kept watch around the maid, and said
She brought her forth, and herself nourished her.

* Compare Æsch. Pers. 186, &c.

But, with compulsion of strong-built device,
The stranger took her, not against her will,
Who heard that Zeus, the ægis-bearing king,
Had fixed by fate Europa for her prize.

Then from her cushioned couch she leapt in fear,
With beating heart ; for as sent straight from heaven
She read this vision : long time on the bed
She sat, and still in her wide-opened eyes
Saw those two women, till at length she spake
After much pause, thus wording timidly :

" Which of the heavenly ones despatched for me
These shady forms ? what dreams are these that came
Flitting about my pillow-pilèd bed
In hours of deep sweet slumber ?—who was she,
That stranger, whom I looked on in my sleep ?
How my heart yearned towards her ! she to me
Beaming a welcome ; as her child, her own,
Regarding me.   Then may the blessèd gods
Order this vision to my future weal !"

So saying, she arose, in haste to find
Her loved companions, equals of her years,
Joy of her heart, and joy of noble sires.
They were her constant playmates, when the dance
Waited her presence ; or when in the gurge
And overflowing of the mountain-brooks
Her fair skin flashed ; or when she fain would stoop
To pluck the odorous lilies of the field.
Full soon they came ; each holding in her hands
A casket to receive the flowery spoil.

Then went they to the ocean-fringing fields,
Where ever they were wont to meet; for there
Profuse-spread roses pleased them; and they heard
Loud echoes of the shoreward rolling wave.
Golden the casket that Europa bore,
Dazzling the eyes, a wonder of the world,
Worked by Hephæstus, and to Libya given
What time she wed the earth-shaking god of sea :
To one of her own kin she sent it on,
Telephaëssa, fairest of the fair,
Who next Europa, her unwedded child,
Dowered with the largess of the priceless gift.
In it shone many a piece of workmanship
Graven with cunning art; in figured gold
There glittered Io, daughter of Inachus,
A heifer still, deprived of woman's form ;
And o'er the briny wastes her wandering feet
Bore her, like some strong swimmer;—there was
                wrought
The blue-black sea, and on a lofty brow
Two men together stood above the shore,
And gazed upon the ocean-ranging beast.
And there was Zeus, with gentle hand divine
Stroking the Inachian changeling, till once more
The broad-horned heifer changed to woman's shape
Beside the seven-streamed courses of the Nile.
Silver the flow of Nile : the heifer shone
In brass ; but Zeus alone was graven of gold.
And round about the spiral casket's rim

Was Hermes; at whose feet in length extreme
Stretched Argus of the ever-wakeful eyes.
And from his deep-dyed blood a bird up-soared,
Carolling exultation at the hue
Of his rich-pictured plumes, and bellying out
Wide pinions, like some swift sea-cleaving ship,
Enfolded with his wings the golden rim.
Such was the casket fair Europa bore.

So, when they reached the many-blossomed meads,
Each sought with ardent joy her favourite flower :
Hyacinths by some, or odorous daffodils
Were culled ; dark violets and balmy thyme
The prize of others ; many a meadow-sweet,
Spring-nurtured, fell to earth ; and others strove
Which first should spoil of his sweet-scented tufts
The yellow crocus ; in their midst the queen,
Choosing the splendour of a fiery rose
Shone radiant, as the foam-born goddess shines
Among the Graces :—little time for her
To dally with sweet flowers ; little time
To guard her virgin zone inviolate ;
For now the son of Chronos bent his eyes
Upon her, till he sank with stricken heart.
Him Cypris with her unregarded darts
Had wounded ; she alone can conquer Zeus.
Then, for he shrank from envious Heré's ire,
And fain would snare the virgin's tender heart,
Shrouding his godhead in a foreign form,
He seemed a bull : no stall-fed ox, nor such

As drags the bent plough through the furrowed glebe ;
Nor such as fattens on lush grass, or yoked
And harnessed draws the heavy-laden wain.
Yellow his body, save where one wide ring
High in mid-forehead glistened silver-white.
Furtively glanced his eyes around, and flashed,
But flashed with gentle kindness ; from his head
His branching horns an equal distance spanned,
As curves the hornèd crescent of the moon,
Her chariot-course half-run.   To the field he came,
Nor ever a one of all the virgin-throng
Trembled to see him, but a great desire
Stirred them to venture near, and gently stroke
The gentle beast.   An odour not of earth
Breathed from him o'er the fields, and far away
Wafted a delicate fragrance.   There he stood
Before Europa, licking her fair neck,
And fixing with his spells the blameless maid,
Who let her hands stray over him, and stooped
To kiss him, and with softest finger-tips
Brushed off the foam that frothed about his jaws.
Then lowèd he in such honied tone, who heard
Would deem he heard no ox, but mellow sounds
Clear-echoed from a crisp Mygdonian flute.
Low at her feet he bowed : Europa still
He fixed his eyes on, and with bended neck
Offered the wide-spread level of his back.
And spake she to the long-haired virgin band :
    " Hither, sweet friends and playmates ! sit we here

Upon this bull; for surely all of us
His mighty back is broadened to support,
Like some strong ship. Kind is he to behold,
And gentle; not at all like other bulls.
The compass of his mind is sound, complete,
As man's is; only is he void of speech."
　　So saying, with a smile she took her seat
High on his back, where they too fain had sat,
The others :—up in an instant sprang the bull,
Possessed of her he longed for; towards the sea
He swiftly strode; and she turned ever round,
And stretched her hands out, calling for her friends
To help her; but they could not make her out.
　　But, when he reached the margin of the shore,
Straightforward, like a dolphin, on he rushed,
Walking the wide waves with unwetted hoofs.
Then sank the sea to calm at his approach,
And whales fore-heralding the path of Zeus
Gambolled around; the dolphin of the abyss
Tumbled above the foam in headlong joy;
Rose from sea-caves the Nereids, and sat
Thick-bevied on the backs of chariot-whales;
And he, the earth-shaking thunderer, ocean king,
Straightened the waves, over the watery way
Guiding his brother; and around him thronged
The peoples of the ever-brimming deep,
Tritons, loud-booming through their spiral conchs,
And hymning a rich bridal melody.
But she, upon the ox-like back of Zeus

Sat, clasping in one hand the branching horn,
And with the other folded from her lap
Her purple-wavy robe, for fear the wash
Of water, and the illimitable sea
Should drench it.   Like the sail of some swift ship,
The bellying breezes filled her deep-fringed vest,
And lightly lifted up the virgin-form.
Then, when her fatherland was far away,
And never sea-girt shore or jutting cliff
Hove into sight, but æther all above,
And all below the immeasurable main,
She murmured, looking wistfully around :
    " What dost with me, god-bull ? and who art thou
That travellest this strange road on heavy feet,
And fearest not the ocean, over which
Swift-wingèd ships may wander to and fro,
But bulls abhor the trackless watery waste ?
Whence shall sweet drink flow for thee ? shall the sea
Furnish thy food ?—or canst thou be a god ?
If not, whence comes the power of godlike deeds ?
Dolphins walk not on land, nor bulls on sea ;
But thou canst tread dry land, and o'er the sea
Roamest with oarage of unwetted hoofs.
Soon, soon, perhaps, above the æthered blue
High-soaring, will thy heavenward flight contend
With storm-swift birds.   Alas, alas for me
Ill-fated, that I left my father's house,
Following this beast, that wiled me to pursue
An unknown voyage and wander all alone !

But thou, O guardian of the hoary deep,
Earth-shaker, meet me with propitious aid !
I see thee, so my hopes blind not my eyes,
Smoothing the waves, and leading me the way
That I should go.   Sure not unhelped of heaven
Could I pass onwards through the watery way."
So said she, and the broad-horned ox replied :
"Maiden, take heart : fear not the ocean-wave.
Lo, I am Zeus himself, albeit I seem
To mortal eyes a bull; for what I will
I make myself appear; strong love for thee
Has made me measure all these ocean-leagues,
Clothed in ox-form ; but now the land of Crete,
Where I myself was reared, shall welcome thee :
There shall be kept with celebration due
Thy marriage rites, and thou shalt have by me
Illustrious sons, a race of sceptred kings,
Ruling each one o'er hosts of mortal men."
      So spake he ; and the god's words were fulfilled.
Soon Crete above the horizon showed ; and Zeus,
Hasting to reassume his form divine,
Loosened the virgin's zone, for whom with care
The happy Hours piled high the bridal bed.
      So she, that erewhile was a simple maid,
Came presently to be the bride of Zeus.

BION.

IDYL I.

The Dirge for Adonis.

DEAD is the fair Adonis; fair Adonis I bewail:
Dead is the fair Adonis; all the Loves take up the
    tale.
O Cytherea, sleep no more in robes of crimson dye;
Arise and shroud thy wretched limbs in dusky dra-
    pery,
And beat thy bosom with thy hands, and far and wide
    deplore:
"My lov'd, my fair Adonis, he is lost for evermore!"

I weep the fair Adonis; to my dirge the Loves
    reply.
He lies upon the mountain ways; the tusk has pierced
    his thigh,
The tooth has torn his lustrous thigh; he gasps his life
    away;
Each parting breath fills Cypris' heart with anguish
    and dismay;

And slowly down his snowy flesh the stream of dark
    blood slips ;
His eyes are glazed beneath their lids ; the rose for-
    sakes his lips.
Gone is the kiss for evermore that seemed to hover
    nigh ;
Dead is the kiss ; but, ah, sad queen, she will not let
    it die !
Still is it sweet to her to kiss, although his life has fled ;
He little knows how many a kiss she wastes upon the
    dead.

Dead is the fair Adonis ; fair Adonis I bewail :
Dead is the fair Adonis ; all the Loves take up the tale.
Deep is the wound that tore his thigh, and bitter is
    the smart ;
But deeper, bitterer the wound in Cytherea's heart.
Howl for their lord his faithful hounds and sadly
    stand beside ;
The mountain Nymphs weep tears for him ; and Cypris
    far and wide
Through the thick oakwoods sad at heart roams with
    dishevelled hair,
Naked her feet, her robes are thin, her flesh the sharp
    thorns tear ;
The sharp thorns pierce her sacred flesh, the blood
    begins to flow ;
Through the long glens with piercing shrieks she
    wanders to and fro,

And cries for her Assyrian spouse, and echoes all her
    woe.

I weep for Cytherea, and the Loves my wail
    resound

    *   *   *   *   *

    *   *   *   *   *

Streams o'er her dainty waist his blood dark welling
    from the wound ;
Her bosom reddens from his thighs ; her breasts, that
    shone before
White as fresh snow, are crimson now with lov'd
    Adonis' gore.

I weep for Cytherea, and the Loves repeat my
    moan.
Lost her fair spouse, and with him lost the beauty
    once her own.
O, long as young Adonis lived, how lovely was her
    grace !
But with his death has likewise died her figure and
    her face.
Ay for Adonis all the oaks and all the mountains cry ;
And ay for Aphrodite's grief the rivers all reply.
And every fountain in the hills weeps for Adonis'
    doom,
And every flower is parched with pain, and shrivelled
    every bloom.

From hill and dale, from brow and brake, her piteous
    voice is sped,
And echo answers hill and dale—" Adonis he is dead!"

I weep for Cytherea ; fair Adonis he is lost.
Who would not weep when Cypris loves—a love so
    sadly crost ?
O, when she knew the fatal wound and saw the mur-
    d'rous dye
Stain his pale limbs, she stretched her arms and cried
    a bitter cry :
"Stay, sad Adonis; stay for me once more to call thee
    mine,
Once more to fold thee in my arms, and mix my lips
    with thine :
Lift up thy head a little space, and give a last long kiss ;
If in a kiss is any life, O be that life in this !
Kiss me till from thy fading soul the last faint breath-
    ings part,
That in my lips they may be caught, and sink into
    my heart ;
That I may drink out all thy love and all thy sweet-
    ness drain,
That I may guard the kiss as though I guarded thee
    again.
For thou, poor love, dost flee away, and far from me
    art gone,
Unto the stern and hateful king and the stream of
    Acheron.

And I, unhappy that I am! must live; I cannot die;
Goddess and queen I may not hope to bear thee company.
O take, Persephoné, my spouse; for thou art mightier far:
All that is fair goes down to thee; with thee I cannot war.
And I must bear my hopeless fate, and bear my quenchless pain;
I can but tremble at thy might, and weep and weep again.
Thou diest, beloved; and like a dream my warm desire has flown,
My home is empty of the Loves, and I am left alone.
And gone with thee my girdle's charm;—O, rash to join the chase!
What frenzied one so fair as thee the fierce wild beasts to face?"

Thus Cypris wailed, and all the Loves gave echo to her moan:
Alas for Cytherea! fair Adonis he is gone.
Fast pours from loved Adonis' thigh a stream of crimson blood,
But faster from the Paphian's eyes descends the briny flood;
And tears and blood take root in earth; from each a flower upgrows;
Her tears beget the anemone; his blood begets the rose.

O Cypris, through the oakwoods dense no more bewail
 thy spouse;
Here is his couch of tender leaves, his bed of forest
 boughs:
His couch and thine; but he is dead, spent is his latest
 breath;
Lovely he lies as though he slept, and beautiful in
 death.
O lay him in the tender robes wherein full many a
 night
He stretched him by thy side and drank of holy sleep's
 delight;
The robes in which he sank to rest upon the golden
 bed,
That too is hateful for its loss, and mourns Adonis
 dead.
Crown him with wreaths and flowrets fair;—the flowers
 have died away,
Died when he died, and lost their bloom, and wasted
 to decay.
With Syrian perfumes bathe his limbs, sprinkle with
 myrrh his head:—
Perish all scents! he was thy myrrh, thy sweet, and
 he is dead.
There in his robes of crimson state the soft Adonis lies,
And all the Loves stand round the bier, and wail with
 piteous cries,
And tear their hair for his sweet sake;—some for his
 arrows go;

One hangs his quiver by his side, and one lays down
    his bow,
And one unties his sandalled shoon, and some in haste
    return,
And carry water from the fount within a golden urn ;
One bathes his limbs, one stands behind, and waves
    his gentle wings,
And fain would wake the dead to life with those soft
    flutterings.

I weep for Cytherea ; to my dirge the Loves reply.
Now Hymen flits from door to door, and bids the
    torchlights die,
And far and wide the nuptial wreaths are scattered in
    the air :
No more to Hymen raise the strain, from songs of joy
    forbear ;
One music only should be heard, a dirge of sad de-
    spair.
Ay for Adonis Hymen weeps, lost, lost, alas, alas !
And the Graces three weep more than he for the son
    of Cinyras.
Dead is the fair Adonis ; each to each takes up the
    tale,
And ay for Cytherea all the Loves repeat the wail.
With shriller shrieks and bitterer tears than ever
    Cypris shed
Mourns for Adonis every Muse, and calls upon the
    dead :

C

" Stay, loved Adonis !" rings their cry ; he answers not
    the strain ;
Fain would he list ; but Proserpine unlooses not his
    chain.

Cease, Cytherea, cease thy wail; enough to-day of
    sorrow ;
Needs store of tears for other years, and a new dirge
    for to-morrow.

TRANSLATIONS

LYRIC AND LATER GREEK POETS.

ALCMAN.

Frag. 21.

No more, young choir of voices honey-sweet,
Soft-singing virgin band, not any more
My limbs can bear me ; O that I had wings,
That I could fly where halcyons fly, and skim
Along the crested blossom of the waves
With careless heart, a sea-blue bird of spring !

Frag. 53.

The mountain-tops are fixed in sleep,
    The dark ravines are still ;
Silent each forward-jutting steep,
    Each torrent from the hill ;
And the forest-leaves, and the creeping things
That out of her bosom the swart Earth brings,
And the beasts that roam on the mountain-side,
And the bees, and the monstrous shapes that hide
    In the secret vaults of the wine-dark deep,
And the birds that fly with their wings stretched wide,
    Tribe after tribe, are hushed in sleep.

ARION.

HIGH god, Poseidon, ocean-king, who hast
The golden trident, and dost girdle round
All earth with zone of thy prolific waves ;
Around thee gambol in unceasing whirl,
With splashing fins, or windy rush of feet
Light bounding onwards, every floating thing,
Flat-nosed, or horrid with thick-bristling mane
Swift-coursing sea-dogs, dolphins loving song,
And whatsoe'er in stormless ocean-halls
Is nurtured by the Nereïd goddess-girls,
Children of Amphitrité.   Once, when I
Was tost in wash of the Sicilian waves,
(For men of guile had hurled me from the ship,
The hollow ship, safe-speeding on its course,
Into the purple bosom of the sea),
Ye took, and bore me rescued to my land—
The land of Pelops, the Tænarian point,
Cleaving the furrows of the Nereïd plain,
And charioting me on your archèd backs
Through all the waste of that unfooted way.

ANACREON.

Frag. 4.

LOVED one, with soft virgin glances beaming,
　Thee I seek; but far away thou strayest,
Never knowing, never dreaming
　That this heart of mine alone thou swayest.

Frag. 44.

Now grizzled are my temples, and white as snow my
　head,
And my teeth are old and useless, and my joyous youth
　has fled;
Short the season yet remaining, and this sweet life will
　be done,
And for this and fear of Tartarus my tears fall one by
　one:
Awful is the hidden Hades, the approach is full of pain,
And whoso once descends shall never more return again.

Frag. 75.

Thracian filly, Thracian filly, why relentless dost thou
　flee,
Looking back askance, and fancying not a grain of
　sense in me?

Think how quickly I could slip the bit and bridle on
    perforce,
Hold the reins, and steer thee deftly round the wind-
    ings of the course.
Now thou feedest in the meadows, now thou leapest in
    light play,
For thou knowest not the traces, and the horseman is
    away!

Frag. 94.

When the full goblet passes, I love not the man who
    can quaff it—
Quaff it, and talk of strife—talk of the horrors of war :
Him do I love, who, adoring the Muses and queen
    Aphrodité,
Mingles their rich bright gifts, mindful of exquisite
    bliss.

ALCÆUS.

Frag. 15.

With brass the whole vast palace gleams,
From floor to roof the solid beams
In honour of Ares all are drest :
Burnished helmets with horse-hair crest
Meet by warriors' brows to be prest;
Dazzling greaves, that fend the brave
From thrust of lance and stroke of glaive,
On pegs unseen above, below,
Are hung; here be breastplates white as snow,
Here too many a hollow shield
Dinted deep in stricken field ;
Swords of Chalcidian forge the boast,
Tunics and doublets, a mighty host.
Since warriors' harness to sing is my aim,
Such goodly gear can I fail to name ?

Frag. 18.

This discord of the winds I cannot fathom :
First from within there comes a monstrous wave,
And then another, also from within.
But we the while and our black ominous bark
Are swept together through the midmost flood,

And greatly struggle with the greater storm :
Where stood the mast the sea comes rushing in,
And every sail is tattered, and great rents
Do show themselves ; the very anchors give.

Frag. 84.

Tell me what ocean-fowl are they,
So swift in flight, in plumage so gay,
That have left the ends of the earth, their home,
On purple wings o'er the deep to roam ?

IBYCUS.

Frag. 1.

THE quince-trees drink new life at early dawn
　　From fountain-heads of many a stream that flows
Beside the virgin's spotless garden-lawn ;
　　And tender vine-shoots under shady boughs
Blossom with tender green :—but not one hour
Of rest for me from Love's almighty power !
Love, like the Thracian north-wind lightning-flashed,
Dark, fearless, and in withering frenzies dashed,
　　From childhood's earliest day
Watches and rules my heart with tyrant sway !

Frag. 2.

Under lids as black as jet
　　Love looks with languishing eyes,
　　And a thousand spells he tries,
Ere he casts me into the net
From whose meshes none ever escapes, I ween,
Who is once entrapped for the Cyprian queen.
But, alas ! when the footsteps of Love draw near,
I can only shake and tremble with fear ;
As the horse, that has often been first in the race,
Is unwilling, when old and worn, to face
The struggle, the crowd, the glowing deeds
Of rushing chariots and harnessed steeds.

PINDAR.

Frag. 106.

FOR them the sun shines with unfading ray
　　Below the realm of night's earth-shading gloom ;
And evermore through happy fields they stray,
　　Where blush-red roses bloom,

And golden fruits abound of every name,
　　And all the air is thick with wafted spice :
Some urge the steed, some seek athletic fame,
　　Some tempt the fickle dice,

And others tune the lyre to joyful measures :
　　But equally to each there does befal
A flower-strewn life of ever-blooming pleasures,
　　Bliss upon bliss to all !

All round this blessèd spot sweet odours rise,
　　From fires that blaze far-seen on many a shrine,
In incense flames of grateful sacrifice
　　To many a power divine !

PLATO.

Frag. 14.

LIGHT of my life ! whene'er thy beauteous eyes
Seek with an upward glance the star-lit skies,
O could I rise on wings of love, and be
That heaven, each star an eye to gaze on thee !

Frag. 15.

Star of the morning shinedst thou
    Ere life had fled :
Star of the evening art thou now
    Among the dead !

Frag. 23.

Here where the woodland thrills with the steadfast
    breath of the west-wind,
Sit near the whispering leaves, sit by the towering pine :
Soon shall my shepherd pipe, and the rivulet plashing
    beside us,
Over thy folded lids draw the enchantment of sleep.

Frag. 30.

Then came we to great breadths of shady copse;
And him, the boy, the son of Cytherea,
The apple-rosy Love, we found within.
No arrow-bearing quiver, no bent bow
Was by him; high in heavy-foliaged trees
They hung: and he the while lay chained in sleep,
Embosomed in a rose's heart of hearts,
And sleeping smiled; and all around his head
And all around his honey-dripping lips
Murmured the yellow workers of the hive.

SAPPHO.

TO APHRODITE.

O SUBTLE queen of many-coloured state,
  Immortal Aphrodité, Zeus-descended,
Crush not my heart, I pray, with such a weight
  Of anguish passion-blended.

But come, if ever once in days gone by
  Thou, listing to my sad voice from afar,
Didst leave thy father's palace at my cry,
  And yoke thy golden car,

And camest, swift sweet sparrows charioteering;
  Mid-air was dense with their innumerous wings
Mazily round dim earth from heaven careering,
  Till stayed their flutterings,

And, with a smile upon thy deathless face,
  Thou didst desire, O blessèd one, to know
Why thus afresh I had invoked thy grace—
  What the new cause of woe,

And what my wild heart craved in all despair:
  "What new Persuasion would thy longing arms
Clasp to the bosom of thy love? Who dare
  To wrong my Sappho's charms?

Ah, she who flies thee now shall soon pursue,
  Who spurns thy gifts shall kneel to thee gift-stored ;
Who loves not, soon to her own heart untrue,
  Shall hail thee her adored !"

Then come again once more, and set me free
  From pangs beneath whose heavy load I bend ;
Accomplish all my heart's desire, and be
  Thyself my guide, my friend !

Frag. 2.

Blest, divinely blest is he
Side by side who sits with thee ;
Side by side who sits so near,
Low sweet whispers he can hear ;
Hear thee, see thee all the while
Smile a loving, longing smile.
At this my fluttering breast rebels,
My heart of hearts in tumult swells.
Soon as I have looked on thee,
Speech no longer comes to me,
All my tongue breaks utterly ;
Straightway courses through my frame
A subtle, all-pervading flame,
And mine eyes can nothing see,
And my ears ring dizzily.

Then in pouring sweat I swim,
Palsy seizes every limb ;
Paler than pale grass I fade ;
Death itself seems scarce delayed.

Frag. 3.

Stars, whene'er the full-orbed moon,
"Riding near her highest noon,"*
Floods with light the land [and sea],
Dim their golden galaxy.

Frag. 93.

Like a ripe red apple
 On the topmost bough,
High above the highest ;
 Who shall pluck it now?

Come the apple-gleaners,
 Let the prize go by ;
Well enough they see it ;
 They cannot reach so high.

* Milton, *Il Penseroso.*

P

SIMMIAS THEBANUS.

Frag. 2.

SPREAD thy pale tendrils out, and gently creep,
Dark ivy, where my Sophocles doth sleep :
There may the rose-leaf and the rose abound,
The vine grape-loaded shed moist shoots around.
Wise was his eloquence ; his honied speech
Each Muse and Grace together joined to teach.

SIMONIDES.

Frag. 4.

WHO at Thermopylæ stood side by side,
And fought together and together died,
Under earth-barrows now are laid in rest,
Their chance thrice-glorious, and their fate thrice-blest:
No tears for them, but memory's loving gaze;
For them no pity, but proud hymns of praise.
Time shall not sweep this monument away—
Time the destroyer; no, nor dank decay.
This not alone heroic ashes holds;
Greece's own glory this earth-shrine enfolds—
Leonidas, the Spartan king; a name
Of boundless honour and eternal fame.

Frag. 27.

When round their carvèd ark the wild winds blew,
 And foaming water filled her soul with fears,
  She, her pale cheeks bedewed with anxious tears,
A mother's arms around her Perseus threw;
  And "O, my child!" she cried,
  "What ills do us betide!
Yet thou sleepest, and with fresh young heart dost
  slumber,
 In this ghastly brazen-banded bark,
Though storm-swept we have been

Through the ebon gloom of night so dark
That its darkness can be seen;
And the waves that roll above us without number
   O'er the tangles of thy long luxuriant hair,
     And the voices of the wind
   Vex not thee, pretty love, lying there
      In thick folds of woollen woof purple-twined.
   But if awe at might divine
     Could chill thee with fear;
   If these mournful words of mine
     Thou hadst power to hear,
I would say: Sleep, infant, sleep;
Be thou hushed, O mighty deep!
Mightier deep of endless woe,
In endless sleep be thou laid low!
And, father Zeus, do thou arrange
Some altered fates, some happier change.
Yet, if my prayers are rash, or passion-wild,
 Forgive the mother, and protect the child!"

Frag. 39.

   Little is the strength of man,
     And his sorrows know no cure;
   Though his life is but a span,
     Trouble comes in sequence sure.
   Death, the while, a grisly shape,
   Hangs o'er all, and none escape:
   Good and bad alike must share;
   Death nor good nor bad will spare.

Frag. 40.

Myriads of birds their way did wing
Over his head when he did sing,
And the fishes out of the dark-blue sea
Leapt right up at his melody.

Frag. 57.

Who, if he thought enough to trust his thoughts,
Would praise Cleobúlus; him, I mean, who dwelt
In Lindus, and against continuance
Of everflowing rivers, and the bloom
Of flowers in spring, and myriad ocean-whirls,
And sparkle of the sun and amber moon,
Pitted the lasting of one poor tombstone?
Why even those, all those, and all things else,
Must yield to power divine :—as for a stone
Men lay their plans, and grind it into dust.
So this intent smacks strongly of a fool.

STESICHORUS.

Frag. 8.

THEN Helios, Hyperion's son, stepped down,
And in the golden bowl embarked, intent
To sail across the Ocean, till he reach
The deep abysmal glooms of reverend Night,
And find his mother, and his wedded wife
And children dear;—but the other, son of Zeus,
Strode on with armèd feet to where the wood
Lies sombre in its myrtle-shaded depths.

ARIPHRON.

ELDEST of the immortal line,
Hygieia, power divine,
What of life is left to me
Grant that I may spend with thee!
Come, O come, with willing heart,
Never, never let us part!
If this life has any pleasure,
Blooming children, hoarded treasure,
Exercise of kingly state
Swaying hosts with equal fate,
Loves and longings deeply hid
Aphrodité's nets amid;
If the Gods send any bliss
Worthy to compare with this;
Any respite from distress,
Any hours of joyousness;
All the gifts each fond Grace showers
In life's radiant spring-time hours,
Bloom and blossom round about thee;
None can happy be without thee.

BACCHYLIDES.

Frag. 28.

HERE are no beeves arranged in ponderous state,
No purple hangings, and no burnished plate :
But friendly temper, and the Muse divine,
And in Bœotian goblets luscious wine.

Frag. 49.

Here in this field Eudemus has raised and devoted a
temple
Sacred to one of the winds, Zephyr, the sweetest of all :
For to his prayers he hearkened, and came to his suc-
cour, and helped him
Out of the mellow ears quickly to winnow the grain.

LYCOPHRONIDES.

Frag. 1.

NOR stalwart sons, nor golden-vestured girls,
Nor e'en rich-bosomed women can command
A face to charm, unless it ever look
Most modest.   For where modesty's the seed,
Beauty doth ever blossom as the flower.

Frag. 2.

This rose I dedicate to thee—
No fairer offering can there be ;
My sandals, and my helmet too,
My spear that erst the wild-beast slew :
My heart is bent on one sweet face,
Dear to each favouring sister Grace.

TIMOTHEUS.

Frag. 10.

Songs of old I will not sing,
 Far better are songs of to-day :
Now the new Zeus he is king,
 Where Chronos erewhile held sway :
 Then, Muse of the past, away !

TRANSLATIONS FROM THE ANTHOLOGY.

MELEAGER.

87.

SWEET is thy harp, yes, by Pan of Arcadia, sweet is its
    music ;
  Crisp and clear is its strain; sweet is it, Zenophila !
How shall I fly from thee ? for on all sides Loves throng
    around me ;
  They will admit no rest,—not for a moment will
    they !
Either thy shape, or thy grace, or thy voice still awakens
    my longing,
  Or thy—what ?—thy all;—all.   I am compassed
    with flame.

92.

Now bloom white violets freshly blown,
    And every scented daffodil
    That drinks soft showers, and on the hill
Dark lilies in profusion thrown.

Now does my love her charms disclose—
    Herself of flowers the loveliest flower—
    Zenophila, as in the bower
Of fond Persuasion blooms a rose.

In vain ye smiling meadows glow
    With blossoms twined among the grass ;
    Since one fair maiden can surpass
Your odorous garlands' fairest show.

O night, O sleepless longings of my heart,
    When I by Heliodora lay !
And O that bitter joy-disturbing smart
    When dimly dawned the untoward day !

Say, does some little love remain for me—
    Say, is there still some tender trace
On the cold couch, to wake a memory
    Of our last passion-warm embrace ?

Say, does she lie all night bedewed with tears ;
    Until, to wile her soul's unrest,
The unbodied semblance of my form appears,
    Clasped fondly to her open breast ?

Or has she some new love, some fresh delight ?
    O lamp that flamest by her side,
Witness not, witness not the heart-breaking sight;
    Guard whom I did to thee confide !

In this garland will I set
Many a snow-white violet ;

The odorous crocus shall be mine,¹
And with myrtles I will twine
Many tender daffodillies,
Many gladsome mountain lilies ;
Purple hyacinths shall be here,
And the rose to lovers dear :
So shall I a wreath bestow
Meet for Heliodora's brow,
And this flower-crown she shall wear
On her clustering perfumed hair.

111.

O, drunk with drops of beaded dew,
    When every other voice is still,
    Thy notes, cicada, echo shrill,
They pierce the woodland through and through.

Thy sharp saw-toothèd feet do rest
    On green leaves high above the ground ;
    Like thrillings of a lyre resound
Strains from thy sun-burnt frame exprest.

I pray thee, chirp such new-born mirth
    For Nymphs whose home is in the trees,
    That thy shrill-woven melodies
May vie with Pan himself in worth.

So I, from Love's enthralling chain
A fugitive, may hope to keep
The noontide hours in quiet sleep,
Stretched out beneath yon shady plane.

112.

Thou that dost beguile my care,
Thou that dost invite soft slumbers,
Rural Muse that all the air
Fillest with shrill-echoing numbers;
Gryllus, gryllus, sing to me;
Sing a love-sick melody;
Let thy little welcome feet
Strike against thy vocal wings,
Till the self-taught woodnotes sweet
Seem a lyre's soft murmurings.
May thy slender-woven strain
Charm away my sleepless pain!
May thy song assuage the smart
Of my passion-wasted heart!
If some guerdon thou shouldst seek,
I will give a blooming leek;
I will give thee, in the morning,
Dew-drops the fresh grass adorning;
Drop by drop, each separate one
Feast for thy small mouth alone!

117.

Child of Tantalus, give ear; listen, Niobe, to me;
Hear the messenger of fate, the piteous tale of misery.
Loose the fillet from thy forehead ;—ah ! that every
    blooming boy
Thou didst bear but for the ruthless darts of Phœbus
    to destroy !
All are gone.—But what is this?—must I behold woe
    piled on woe?
All around, alas, alas ! the tide of virgin blood doth
    flow ;
One sinks at her mother's knees ; within her lap one
    seeks a nest ;
One is stretched upon the ground ; and one still hangs
    upon her breast;
One in stupor faces death; another crouches in affright
From the arrow ; one just living sees the last faint
    gleam of light.
And she, whose tongue so loved to boast, now linger-
    ing all alone,
Stands fixed, unhappy mother, and is frozen into stone.

124.

Piteously weeping, thy mother, Charixenus, gave thee
    to Hades ;
    Eighteen years didst thou bloom; then must thy
      robe be thy shroud.

Surely a stone would have wept when, away from the
  halls of thy fathers,
    Friends of thy own young years mournfully carried
      thy corpse :
Dismally wailed the women, instead of a chant
  hymeneal;
    Ah! for the breast where he hung; why was its
      sweetness in vain ?
Why were such travail-throes all in vain? Ah! fate
  unpropitious,
    What boots a mother's love? Lo, it is tost to the
      winds.
Now must his parents weep, and his fond companions
  lament him ;
    Strangers who hear the sad tale tribute of pity
      bestow.

PAUL THE SILENTIARY.

8.

Though thy brow is wrinkled over,
Dear is each line to thy lover,
Dearer than all earth's young faces
Beaming with a thousand graces.

Though like ripe fruit droops thy bosom,
    Let me fold it in my arms,
Sooner than each firm breast-blossom
    Crowning the proud virgin's charms.

More thy waning autumn charms me
    Than another's springtide gay ;
More thy winter sunshine warms me
    Than another's summer ray.

EVENUS.

3.

SOME folk, whatever you may say,
　Will go on arguing, you may trust 'em;
But arguing in the proper way
　By no means is their usual custom.

There is an old and homely saw,
　The very thing such strife to smother:
" Good sir, the end of all your jaw
　Is—you think one way, I another."

You'll soon convince, if you are right,
　All who can false from true discern;
For those who know the most are quite
　The first, the readiest to learn.

13.

Airy sprite near Athens bred,
Swallow on sweet honey fed,
Thou dost chirp and snatch away
One that chirps like thee all day,
And carriest to thy callow brood
The cicale for their dainty food.
Thou dost chatter, so does he,
Winged alike for flight are ye :

Thou dost skim the Attic strand,
He knows not another land :
Thou dost love the summer sun ;
When it fades, *his* life is done;
Haste, then, haste, and set him free ;
Right and just it cannot be
That thou shouldst end his little strain—
A songster by a songstress slain !

14.

I was that city once, far seen of men,
Ilion the sacred, much renowned for walls
Decked with fair coronal of towers ; but now
The dust and ashes of unnumbered years
Have all devoured me.   Still am I enshrined
In Homer : there the gates that shut me in
Are banded with irrefragable brass :
There no Achæan spears shall reach to pierce
And ravage me ; but I shall live and lie
Upon the tip of every Hellene tongue.

15.

Neither too much nor too little 'tis good to partake of
    the wine-cup ;
  Thence mad passions arise, thence comes a future
    of woe.
Happy who quaffs his share, with three fair nymphs to
    attend him ;

Then may he sink to rest ready, ay, ready for love.
But if he reeks of drink, lo! the little Loves will
    desert him ;
Soaked, he shall wallow in sleep—sleep, a near
    neighbour of death !*

---

* Vina parant auimum Veneri, nisi plurima sumas,
    Et stupeant multo corda sepulta mero :
  Aut nulla ebrietas, aut tanta sit, ut tibi curas
    Eripiat: si qua est inter utramque, nocet.
                            OVID. *Rem. Amoris,* 806, &c.

EURIPIDES.

CRESPHONTES. Frag. 15.

RICHLY dowered with treasures rarest,
Peace, of happy gods the fairest,
For thee I long. Yet much I fear,
Ere thy lingering steps draw near,
Under whelming weight of woe
Wintry age may lay me low,
Ere I see thy joyous face,
Ere I see thy youthful grace,
And the mingled dance and song
Of the flower-crowned festive throng.
Come, goddess, come ; drive far away
The feuds that waste our homes to-day ;
The maddening strife that will not feel
Joy in aught but clashing steel.

ERECHTHEUS. Frag. 13.

Lie by, my spear; round arms of mine
Their silvery threads let spiders twine ;
Let peace and peaceful arts engage
The years of my declining age.
O, let me sing, my hoary head
With myrtle-wreaths engarlanded ;
And hang in my Athenian home
Threïcian shield 'neath pillared dome ;
And written voices strive to unfold
The words of famous men of old.

PHILOSTRATUS.

THE ISLAND OF ACHILLES.*

PHŒNICIAN.

BUT tell me what that strange tale was that Protesilaus knew about the island in the Pontic sea; for it was in some such place that he met with Achilles.

VINE-DRESSER.

It was, my friend; and he gives this account of it: that among the islands of that sea there is one situate more towards its barrenest side, which those who make the entrance to the sea keep on their left hand. Its length is thirty furlongs, its breadth not more than four. Trees grow on it,—poplars and elms; the elms here and there as they will, the poplars round a shrine in rows. The shrine is built facing the lake Mæotis, which is of bulk equal to the sea, and debouches into it. And in the shrine are statues—Achilles and Helena joined together by the Fates. Now the eyes are the seat of love, and from the eyes poets draw their songs of love; yet Achilles and Helena, who had never even seen each other,— for she was in Egypt, and he before Ilion, — were driven from the first to love each other, their ears being creators of their desire. And since the Fates

---

* With regard to the island of Achilles compare Euripides, *Andromache*, 1260, &c.; Maximus Tyrius, xv. 7; Stephanus Byzant. *de Urbibus*, p. 147.

had decreed to them immortality, and there was no
fit island near Ilion, and the Echinades, lying towards Œniadæ and Acarnania, were polluted (for Alc-
mæon had slain his mother, and was dwelling in the
delta of the Acheloüs, that had grown up even since
his crime), Thetis prayed Poseidon to make rise out
of the sea some island, in which they could dwell.
And he thought over the length and breadth of the
sea, and how—for there was no island therein—ships
sailed over it, and saw no living soul; and he caused
to appear the island Leucé, whereof I have spoken,
that Achilles and Helena might dwell therein, and
that sailors might rest there and drop their anchors in
the deep. And sole sovereign as he was of the whole
watery kingdom, he looked upon the rivers,—the
Thermodon, the Borysthenes, and the Ister,—and
thought what immeasurable and ever-flowing waters
they roll into the sea; and he caused the *débris* of
the rivers, which, from their source in Scythia, they
carry down with them to the sea, to deposit itself;
and therefrom he shaped the island whereof I spoke,
and planted it firmly in the ocean. And there for
the first time Achilles and Helena saw and embraced
each other. And Poseidon himself and Amphitrité
celebrated their marriage, and all the Nereïds, and
all the gods of rivers and streams that flow into
lake Mæotis and the sea. And in that island there
are water-fowl, white of wing, and with a savour of
the sea, whom Achilles has made to minister to him;

and they add a charm to his shady retreat, fanning a gentle breeze with their wings, and scattering dewy showers from their feathers. And this they do by first flitting low along the ground, and then hovering at a little height overhead. And this island is holy to touch at for mortals sailing to the ocean-gorge, and ships greet it as a friendly haven; but not the less are all voyagers forbidden to tarry on it, Hellenes as well as foreigners from the coasts of the sea. And when they have cast anchor, and offered at the shrine, they must embark again at sunset, and stay not the night on shore, but sail away, if the breeze favours, and if not, lay the vessel at moorings, and rest in the hold. For then is it said that Achilles and Helena banquet together, and indulge in song, chanting their mutual loves, and the poems of Homer about Troy, ay, and Homer himself. For the gift of poesy, with which Calliopé visited Achilles, he still holds in much esteem, and is zealous about it the more now that he rests from the battle. And believe me, friend, the hymn in honour of Homer is a divine composition, and of true poetic spirit.

PHŒNICIAN.

Might I hear this hymn; or is it forbidden to repeat it?

VINE-DRESSER.

Surely, friend, many of those who touch at the island say that they are wont to hear Achilles singing

many and divers melodies. But this hymn, that was,
as I believe, composed last year, is especially graceful
in its feeling and conception. It runs thus :

" By the infinite water dwelling,
    Over the bounds of the mighty sea,
When the notes of the lyre are swelling,
    Echo, my fingers awaken thee.
Sing, then, sing me Homer the divine,
    Him who crowns heroic names with glory ;
Him through whom those many toils of mine
    Live in story.
I shall not die, in him I live,
    In him my lov'd Patroclus breathes again ;
In him my godlike Ajax does survive,
And Ilion, mourned in many a measured strain,
Shall still exalt its spear-won towers on high,
Shall endless fame inherit, and never, never die !"

       *   *   *   *   *   *

    The songs heard in the island are of this wise,
and the voice that sings them sounds clear and as the
voice of a god. And its notes reach so far out to sea
that sailors quake and tremble with consternation.
And those that cast anchor near the island report that
they hear the trampling of horses, and the clash of
armour, and the cry of battle. And if, when wishing
to anchor at the north or south of the island, a con-
trary wind should hinder them from letting go, then
does Achilles appear to them on the prow, and com-

mands them to shift their position and to give way to the wind. And many that are wont to voyage in this sea come to me and report these things, and, by Zeus, if only they get a glimpse of the island, they embrace each other as men who have been belated in an illimitable ocean, and weep for very joy. And when they have reached it and saluted the shore, they go to the shrine, and offer prayer and sacrifice to Achilles. And the victim, that has been supplied according to the size of the ship and the means of the sailors, stands of its own accord by the altar.

*　　*　　*　　*　　*　　*

And Achilles is reported to have appeared to a merchant who was in the habit of passing and repassing the island, and to have narrated the tale of Troy, and to have kept him company in a flagon of wine, and to have commanded him to sail thence to Ilion, and bring him back a Trojan girl, mentioning her by name, and mentioning by name one in Ilion whose slave she was. And when this merchant, from astonishment at the request, asked him (for he had acquired confidence) what need he had of a Trojan slave, Achilles answered, "Because, my friend, she was born of the race whence Hector and Hector's forefathers sprang; and she is the sole relic of the blood of Priam and the descendants of Dardanus." So the merchant fancied that Achilles was in love, and went, and purchased the girl, and sailed back to the island. And Achilles commended him for coming, and commanded him to keep the girl for him in the ship (for, as I believe, no woman might set foot on the island), but to come himself at eventide to the shrine, and to feast with him and with Helena. And at eventide he went, and Achilles gave him many gifts that merchants have not, and bade him welcome, and promised him a successful venture, and a prosperous voyage. And when day dawned, "Take these gifts," he said, "and get thee hence, and set sail, and leave the girl upon the shore to await my coming." And when scarce a furlong from the shore there came to him shrieks of pain from the girl, for Achilles was tearing her in pieces, and rending her limb from limb.

The End.

LONDON:

LOBBON AND SON, GREAT NORTHERN PRINTING WORKS,
PANCRAS ROAD, N.W.

www.ingramcontent.com/pod-product-compliance
Lightning Source LLC
Chambersburg PA
CBHW030404270326
41926CB00009B/1258